Monty's
Grandfather

In memory of
my darling wife Bunty

Monty's Grandfather

Sir Robert Montgomery, GCSI, KCB, LLD 1809-1887

A Life's Serivce for the Raj

Brian Montgomery

BLANDFORD PRESS
POOLE · DORSET

First published
in the U.K. 1984
by Blandford Press,
Link House
West Street, Poole, Dorset, BH15 1LL

Copyright © *1984 Brian Montgomery*

Distributed in
the United States by
Sterling Publishing Co., Inc.,
2 Park Avenue, New York,
N.Y. 10016

British Library Cataloguing in Publication Data

Montgomery, Brian
  Monty's grandfather.
  1. Montgomery, *Sir* Robert
  I. Title
  325'.341'0954   DS481.M/

ISBN 0 7137 1401 8

Typeset in 10/11 pt. Compugraphic Garamond
by Graphicraft Typesetters Ltd.
Printed in Great Britain by
Biddles Ltd., Guildford.

Contents

Acknowledgements

The author and publisher wish to thank the publishers and copyright holders of the books which are listed in the Bibliography for their permission to reprint extracts from their works, with particular thanks to: Anthony Sheil Associates Ltd (Mason, P. *A Matter of Honour* (Jonathan Cape) © 1974 by Philip Mason), Oxford University Press (Smith, V. *The Oxford History of India* 4th ed, 1981) and Asia Publishing House Ltd (Raj, Dr Pragdish *The Mutiny and British Land Policy in North India* 1965).

The main sources of information and illustrations in this biography stem from my grandfather's private papers. In addition, Sir Robert had spoken frequently about his experiences in India to Bishop Montgomery, who meticulously recorded much of their conversation in his own handwriting, and also in his (unpublished) short history of Sir Robert. I was fortunate to have the benefit of these family sources during the long hours that I spent with the Bishop while he talked about his father. These reminiscences were particularly valuable in their wealth of detail about conditions in the North Western Provinces, the Punjab, and in Oudh and Lucknow, during the twenty or so years preceding the outbreak of the Sepoy Mutiny in 1857.

This story could not have been completed without the advantage of wide research to check its historical accuracy, particularly where personal memories have been responsible for much detail and description. I therefore owe much to other sources and which I gratefully acknowledge below.

First and foremost I owe so much to my wife, who read each page in draft as it was finished and provided invaluable correction and stimulating comment. As always, I am particularly grateful to my stepson Tom MacNeece who, as a journalist, cast a professional eye over my work to avoid the pitfalls of repetition and lack of brevity.

ACKNOWLEDGEMENT

I owe a deep debt of gratitude to all the staff at the India Office Library and Records for their unfailing help and encouragement, not only in tracing and providing invaluable books and other research material, without which I could not have filled in many gaps in my background knowledge, but also for the ever ready technical assistance, especially in photocopying, that I was so freely given. In this context I wish particularly to thank Dr R.J. Bingle and Mr A.J. Farrington for their whole hearted support. My sincere thanks are also due to Mrs P. Rohatgi, Mrs K. Bell, Mr A. Cook and Mr G. Armitage for providing essential prints and maps, and to Mr S. Quraishi and Mrs A. Commander for translation of vernacular texts and other advice.

I made frequent and profitable visits to the London Library, where the staff were always so kind and attentive in guiding my footsteps to look for material in that maze of historic documentation. I have equal cause for gratitude to the staffs at the London Library and at the Public Record Office, where I should have been quite helpless without expert assistance in the computerised record system.

I wish to thank the staff at the Library of the Church Missionary Society, the School of Oriental and African Studies, and the Indian Army Room at the Royal Military Academy, Sandhurst, for their unfailing assistance.

My gratitude is more than ever due to Ronald Lewin for so much wise counsel and advice, and particularly for his public support of my project in the Foreword he has so generously provided.

I was most fortunate in having the professional indexing skill of Miss Ann Hoffman, who so promptly produced an admirable index, and of Tom Hartman for his literary advice at all stages.

I owe a very great deal to Miss Sheena Barber and Miss Susan Cowley for their hard work and skills in typing this whole work; their patience in putting up with my repeated requests for re-drafting and their quick perception of my clerical mistakes were quite invaluable; in this context I wish also to thank Mrs Walker of Peter Coxson Limited, for so promptly coming to my rescue when time was running short.

I shall always recall with deep gratitude the visit I was able to pay to the Director of the National Archives of New Delhi, who so generously guided my research in his records.

I have to thank my publishers, and particularly Mr Stuart Booth, for their expert guidance and advice at all stages in the production of the book including their care in the vetting of my account.

Finally, none of the sources I have mentioned are responsible for any errors of fact or omission which may remain, and for which I am responsible, including the views expressed in this book, which are my own.

Foreword

by
Ronald Lewin

Robert Montgomery was one of the rocks on which the waves of the Indian Mutiny broke and lost their menace. But one is grateful that his correspondence and intimate papers survived so casually at the family home in Ireland, until they came into the hands of a grandson capable of giving them a new life, because they remind one of how vast a dominion was administered by how few men. Montgomery himself, the great Lawrence brothers, John Nicholson - even if one adds the smaller fry, a condottiere, say, like Hodson of Hodson's Horse - 'the founders' (as Philip Woodruff christened them in his classic evocation *The Men Who Ruled India*) were incredibly few on the ground.

And they were hard men. Colonel Montgomery's generous but relentless quotations from the letters that passed between the founders show that the Victorian ethic and the confident Victorian trust in God which drove them on owed more, in spirit, to the Old Testament than to the New. There is a famous sentimental passage by George Santayana about the Englishman: 'He carries his English weather in his heart wherever he goes, and it becomes a cool spot in the desert . . . Never since the heroic days of Greece has the world had such a sweet, just, boyish master.' It was not quite like that in the Punjab under the Lawrences and Montgomery, nor would they have wished it to be.

Paternalism, certainly: building roads and bridges, improving agriculture, keeping the peace, quelling corruption, daily imposing the law. But it is most interesting to read in these pages, in the words of the founders themselves, how their immense commitment to getting things done and getting things right made more room for a sense of duty than for love. It seems a harsh creed. Yet we are also reminded here, by the participants themselves, of the savage story of the Mutiny and the fact that it was the very quality of that commitment, the devotion to duty above all, which enabled them to keep their nerve.

Duty, severity: for some readers there will be a distasteful aspect. Firing sepoys alive from guns is scarcely an acceptable procedure, not to be performed, perhaps, by Christian gentlemen even when their wives and children are being slaughtered, their life's work is in jeopardy, and the British presence in india is apparently at risk. The mutineers in Delhi did the same thing, of course, to their own kind. A calmer view suggests that the convention of one age becomes the bestiality of the next. It also raises the question whether the generation that bombed Hamburg and Dresden, that roasted Hiroshima and spread its napalm over Vietnam has much of a *locus standi* in this matter.

A later Victorian, putting the words in the mouth of an imaginary Burman, wrote: 'When we see two or three Englishmen alone governing a great district, you appear to us not individuals but tiny finger-tips of a great living thing whose heart and brain are far away.' This is true of Montgomery and all the founders, and the great living thing was the East India Company, that complex organisation whose vital centre was far away in London. But there was another nexus: the family. It is touching and surprising to read how Montgomery not only maintained his own household's stability amid all the distractions of his professional career but also, by constant interchange of correspondence, was never out of touch with the Irish home and the Irish roots. No air letters or telephones for the founders! Yet the umbilical cord never snapped.

Colonel Montgomery's own sense of family - Robert had a Bishop for a son, and a Field Marshal for a grandson - has not caused him to forget that he is not writing ancestor worship but, granted the material at his disposal, an important contribution to the history of India. On the contrary. In his concluding pages he asks whether the founders were really men sent from God to govern their inferiors, as they believed, and whether Britain was right to maintain this attitude so persistently. His answer sets the seal on a fine book, for it is the answer of a man without prejudice.

Sir Robert Montgomery
GCSI, KCB, LLD

1809, 2nd Dec.	*Born*: At New Park, Moville, Co. Donegal, Ireland. *Father*: The Rev. Samuel Law Montgomery, BA, LLB Rector of Moville. *Mother*: Susan Maria McClintock of Trintaugh, Co. Donegal, and widow of the Rev. Mounsey Alexander who died 1790.
1817–1824	Educated at Foyle College, Londonderry
1824–1825	Cadet of the Military College of the East India company at Addiscombe.
1826–1828	Wraxhill Hill School, Yorkshire.
1828	Commissioned in the Bengal Engineers of the East India Company's military service.
1828	Transferred to the Civil Service of the East India Company.
1828, 30th May	Left New Park, Moville, by sea for service in India.
1828, 13th Nov.	Disembarked at Calcutta to begin service as a writer in the Bengal Civil Service.
1829, Dec.	Appointed Assistant Magistrate, and Collector, Azamgarh.
1834, 17th Dec.	Married Frances Mary, daughter of the Rev.

	James Thomason of the Bengal Ecclesiastical Service.
1835	Appointed Magistrate, and Collector, Azamgarh.
1837, April	Appointed Magistrate, and Collector, Allahabad.
1842, 23rd Mar.	Frances Mary Montgomery died, and buried, at Allahabad.
1843, 12th Jan.	Sailed from Calcutta for three years furlough in UK.
1845, 2nd May	Married Ellen Jane, daughter of William Lambert Esq. of Woodmansterne, Surrey.
1846, Jan.	Returned to India as Magistrate and Collector Cawnpore.
1848, Mar.	Appointed Commissioner of Lahore Division at Lahore.
1851	Appointed Member of Board of Administration for Punjab.
1853-1858	Appointed Judicial Commissioner The Punjab.
1858-1859	Appointed Chief Commissioner Oudh.
1859-1865	Appointed Lieutenant Governor The Punjab.
1865	Returned to the UK on retirement.
1865	Appointed Member of the Secretary of State of Council for India.
1887, 28th Dec.	Died at 7 Cornwall Gardens, London, SW1. Buried in Londonderry Cathedral.

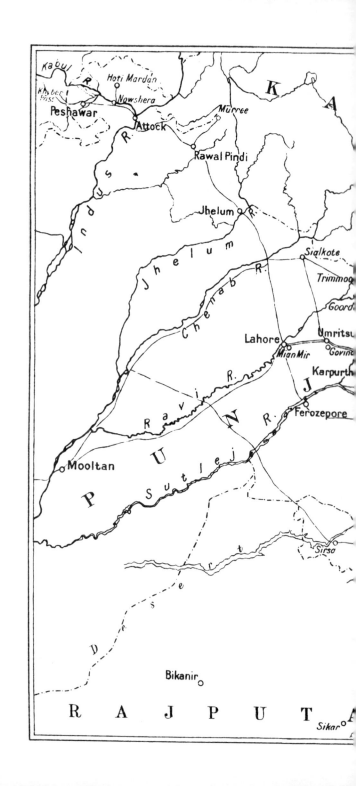

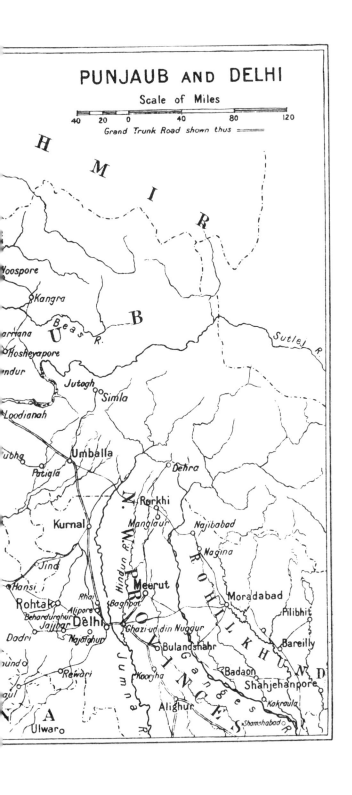

PUNJAUB AND DELHI

Scale of Miles

40 20 0 40 80 120

Grand Trunk Road shown thus ═══

H
M
I
R
B
U

Noospore

Kangra

Beas R.

arriana

Hosheyapore

ndur

Jutogh

Simla

Loodianah

Sutlej R.

ubha

Umballa

Patiala

Dehra

Rurkhi

Kurnal

Manglaur

Najibabad

Jind

Nagina

Hansi

Meerut

Rhai

Baghpot

Moradabad

Rohtak

Alipore

Pilibhit

Behardurghur

Jajjur

Delhi

Ghazi-ud-din Nuggur

Dadri

Najafghur

Bulandshahr

Bareilly

nundo

Rewari

Koorjha

Badaon

Shahjehanpore

aul

Alighur

Kakraula

Ulwar

Shamshabad R.

A

N

D

Hindun R.

N.W. PROVINCES

ROHILKHUND

Jumna

Ganges

A GENERAL MAP
OF INDIA AND BURMA

l
a   y   a   s

E *P* *A* *L*
G *U* *R* *K* *H* *A* *S*

Patna
R Ganges   Murshidabad
haksar
Plassey

Calcutta

Bay of
Bengal

Rangoon

Andaman
Islands

O   C   E   A   N

Introduction

In the late spring of 1848 Lord Dalhousie, the Governor-General of India, was in camp at Allahabad in the North-Western Provinces. The camp was sited beyond the western outskirts of the city, where the residential suburbs with the Civil Lines and the military cantonment now stand. It covered acres of ground on which thousands of men and women were accommodated in tents and shelters of every kind. There were carriages and horses galore, with more than twenty elephants, scores of camels both for state occasions and for transportation, and many hundreds of bullocks for the ox-carts which were needed to convey great quantities of baggage. For when the Governor-General was on tour he took with him the ceremonial trappings of his high office, in order to maintain all the immense grandeur and dignity of the British raj, together with imposing evidence of its military power. He would be meeting Hindu Maharajahs and Muslim Nawabs who ruled their own states and had large armies, and who might turn out to meet him with thousands of troops and dozens of elephants.

On this occasion Lord Dalhousie's own escort consisted of a battery of European Horse Artillery with a battalion of British infantry, a regiment of regular Bengal Cavalry, and another of Bengal Native Infantry, and of course the Governor-General's mounted Bodyguard in their brilliant scarlet uniforms with dark blue facings and silver lace, and wearing their distinctive head-dress - a black shako with long black horsehair plume. Finally there were the heads and staff of at least three departments of the civil government of India at Calcutta, whose work had to continue but required the presence of the person who represented both Her Majesty The Queen and the Court of Directors of the Honourable The East India Company. From this camp the following letter was dispatched by the private office of the Governor-General.

INTRODUCTION

Governor-General's Camp
Allahabad

12th March 1848

My dear Thomason,
 Will you order up Montgomery from Cawnpore immediately? He will be a Commissioner of some sort, probably of the Lahore Division, on Rupees 2,400 a month - the Board of Administration will consist of the two Lawrences and Mansel.

Yrs. sincerely,
H. W. Elliot

P.S. The G.G. will not declare his policy yet but within a fortnight I fancy you will receive a public letter calling for the selected Civilians. He will not take Temple.[1]

 The letter was signed by Sir Henry Elliot, Secretary to Lord Dalhousie, and was addressed to Mr James Thomason, Lieutenant-Governor of the North-Western Provinces, at Agra.
 Anyone reading this letter, written so long ago, might wonder who this Mr Montgomery was? To be appointed personally by the Governor-General in this fashion must mean that he was a senior official; for he was to work with the Board of Administration of the newly-created province of the Punjab, in close association with two already famous men, Sir Henry Lawrence and Sir John Lawrence. At that time his name was certainly unknown in England outside East India House in London. But matters did not remain so, for eleven years later, on 14th April 1859, Parliament at Westminster resolved that the thanks of both the House of Lords and of the House of Commons should be conveyed to Sir Robert Montgomery, GCSI, KCB, LLD, in recognition of his services for the re-establishment of peace in Her Majesty's Indian Dominions. In the years that followed he became Lieutenant-Governor of the Punjab, and finally for twenty years a member of HMG's Council of India at Whitehall. A large district in the Punjab and its capital town were both named 'Montgomery' in his memory. His active professional service in India and in London (for he never retired, and died in harness) lasted for fifty-nine years. There are memorials to him in the cathedrals at Lahore and Londonderry, and in the Crypt of St. Paul's[2], in the City of London, there is an inscribed plaque of white marble, in the form of his medallion portrait, carved by Bruce Joy. In the Foreign and Commonwealth Office at Westminster his marble bust, by the same sculptor, stands on a plinth in a main corridor of the first floor, and his full length portrait, painted by Sir Francis Grant, hangs in one of the Secretary of State's offices.
 Robert Montgomery, an Irishman born and bred, was the second son of

the Rector of Moville in Co. Donegal in the Republic of Ireland. His mother was Susan Maria McClintock, whose family came from Trintaugh in the same county. The origins of both these Protestant families stem from King James I's Plantation of Ulster early in the seventeenth century, when much Irish land and property were 'conveyed' to settlers from Scotland. The Montgomerys had settled in Co. Donegal and bought an estate there, and later founded a prosperous wine and spirits business in Londonderry, which closed down when Robert's father was ordained a clergyman. So many families, still in the nine counties of the old Ulster, have similar backgrounds, and it is remarkable how often their members contributed to the growth and development of the British Empire in India.

Apart from his long professional career, my grandfather led a most eventful life, with many vicissitudes, including the fact that, like his mother, he was twice married and had many children. In his day people had ample time to write long letters, which were generally kept by their recipients. Robert certainly retained all the letters he received during his long years in India, both in his official and private capacity, together with the voluminous records of previous generations of his family. All this mass of manuscript paper, with much cross-writing which was always difficult to read, had been kept loose in large leather travelling trunks, without any attempt at filing or indexing. It must have remained thus, untouched, for well over half a century, from the time Robert finally left India, until 1920 when his son, Bishop Montgomery, my father, recovered it from the stables at New Park, our family home in Moville. Lady Montgomery, Robert's widow, had just died aged ninety-five. She had never mentioned the existence of this material to any member of her family, though she outlived her husband by thirty-two years. So the Bishop set about the task of sorting and indexing the documents, many of which he recognised as having great historical interest and value. Before he died in 1932 he wrote: 'It is too late in the day to publish the record of my father's life'.

Once again the papers were moved across the world, to Kenya, where my eldest brother was the Chief Native Commissioner, until they came to rest in England in the large barn at Isington Mill, then the home of my third brother the late Field-Marshal Viscount Montgomery of Alamein. Unfortunately by this time one of the volumes had suffered serious damage, a large slice of it having been eaten by mice. I well remember the day, some years ago, when the Field-Marshal gave me these records, and how impressed I was by the story they reveal.

Sir Robert Montgomery's papers are now to be part of the collection of private papers in the India Office library, now merged with the British Library in London. The library have confirmed that they will represent a very important addition to their archives and to the records of this period of British rule in India. There is much new material about controversial events, before, during, and after the great sepoy mutiny of 1857, in the form of original reports and letters by famous men and women of those times. The papers, which have been the source and inspiration for this book, also describe the work and life, with all its hardships, loneliness and dangers, as well as the pleasures and pastimes, of a civil officer in the service of the government of India, who began his career there in the last two years of the reign of King George IV. Sir Robert was by no means always successful and at times he was heavily criticised by the press in India, and by members of his own staff, who objected strongly to his policy. At the height of his career he was very nearly sacked, but he managed to survive. His story also includes the fortunes, good and bad, of his family, and is accompanied by original photographs dating from the eighteen-fifties.

I
India Ahead

My grandfather Robert Montgomery was born on 2nd December 1809 at New Park, his family home in Inishowen, that wild and remote region of Co. Donegal which lies between Lough Foyle and Lough Swilly. His father, Samuel Law Montgomery, had been ordained a priest and was the Rector of his local parish of Moville, as well as the owner of a small estate that included all the land on which the popular seaside resort and town of Moville now stands. However, in those days Moville was only a small hamlet, and the ground on which there is now a market place with shops and a residential area, was all farmland; the parish church of Moville was then at Greencastle, at the mouth of Lough Foyle two and a half miles from the Rector's home. So Robert Montgomery grew up in a very sparsely-populated area and was essentially a country man, conditioned by the strictly religious atmosphere of a small parish in the Protestant Church of Ireland - then as now, a minority living in the midst of a predominantly Roman Catholic community.

Compared with our times, life there 170 years ago was very simple. Apparently meat in that part of Ireland was little eaten; for Robert wrote in his papers that: 'We had meat at New Park on Sundays only. At times a man would call to say he had "a view of a sheep. Would the Rector take a joint if he killed?"' I was surprised also by Robert's record that the country people of Inishowen ate very few potatoes, which in those days were by no means a staple diet. Outside the towns and big villages they lived on oatmeal porridge and oat bread, and drank buttermilk, nor was tea drunk except as a luxury. Every farmer grew his own wool; the girls spun it and were called spinners (spinsters) in consequence. Boots then were a luxury, and girls frequently had one pair between two, to be put on outside the town or village and taken off when returning home. Otherwise

1

the girls seldom wore shoes or stockings, always shawls, and never hats. Another observation Robert noted concerned the visits he and his brothers and sisters frequently made to the country folk in Moville or Greencastle, where chairs or stools were always provided 'for the squire's children'. These were first cleaned with human spittle for them to sit on! Inside the cottages pigs and poultry lived on the earthen floor (hens sometimes shared the family bed!) and there was a turf fire which was never allowed to go out.

This was the countryside in which Robert Montgomery spent his early boyhood until in 1817, when, just eight years old, he was sent to school as a boarder at Foyle College in Londonderry, where the life certainly inured him to hardship and taught him how to fight for himself.

In those days Derry City had not spread much beyond its walls and the 'New Free Grammar School' (as Foyle College was then called) stood in open country outside. The school grounds were large, and covered all the area between the present Northlands Road and where the Asylum used to be. There were one hundred and ten pupils of whom half were boarders, and they were all taught in one large schoolroom without any divisions between classes or age groups. The college was described in its charter as 'Primarily a Classical School', and pupils were shown on the college roster as being either 'at Latin', for those aspiring to become university graduates, or 'at English' for all others. Robert was 'at Latin' and so also was John Lawrence (later Viceroy of India) though neither of them ever went to a university. There were five Lawrence brothers (Alexander, George, Henry, John and Richard) at Foyle College and it was there that the Lawrence-Montgomery association began and continued during their lifetime; all five Lawrence brothers will appear in this book as no account of my grandfather's life would be complete without them.

The three elder Lawrence boys had arrived at the school, as boarders, in the winter of 1816, and were very soon involved in the 'school battle'. This was a perpetual war waged between the boarders and day-boys for possession of an ancient fortress which stood high on a hill behind the school building. A year later the three were joined by Robert Montgomery and John Lawrence in defence of the earthwork against raids made day and night, summer and winter, by the day-boys. Both sides challenged the other 'to come out and fight now'. The contest was hard and savage with a variety of weapons like cabbage stalks (kale runts), empty whisky barrels rolled down on the attackers during their night assualts, and hurley sticks for hand-to-hand combat. It was astonishing that serious injuries were apparently few and far between, which can only mean that the boys on each side were extremely tough and vigorous.

In school the Headmaster, the Reverend James Knox (he was an uncle of the Lawrence brothers), was a stern disciplinarian, and flogging was the order of the day. In addition there was very strict religious training, both in and out of school hours, from which there was little hope of escape. The Headmaster's sister had this part of the education as her special charge; she used to send for the boys every two or three days, one by one and always during their spare time, in order that she might read and pray with them. The Lawrences, being nephews as well as pupils, got a double dose of this treatment, and Robert Montgomery recorded how they used to slink by their aunt's room, on tiptoe, in the hope of escaping. But it was of no avail; for the door would open and their aunt would pounce out on them and carry them off to a lecture – on their great need of prayer and repentance!

Years later, it was Christmas Eve 1851, three Foyle College old boys, Henry and John Lawrence and Robert Montgomery, all then in their early forties, were dining together at Lahore, where the two Lawrences, with Robert, were jointly responsible for government of the Punjab. After dinner Robert said to the other two: 'I wonder what the old Simpsons are doing in Derry. I suggest we send them a joint Christmas present; I will give £50 (a large sum by any standards in those days) if you two will do the same.' Both agreed at once, for the Simpsons were twin brothers (William and Robert) who had been masters at Foyle College and had taught the three men. The twins were famous in their day, but very simple people, risen as it were from the ranks with virtually no educational training, and probably a butt among the boys in their classes; but they were fanatical in their loyalty to Foyle and their regard for its pupils. Later George Lawrence, then Political Agent in Rajputana, also contributed £50, so a joint letter trom the four old boys, with a cheque for £200, was sent to the Simpson twins. After many months an answer came in a delightfully naive reply, which began: 'My dear boys' – then 'boys' was scratched out and 'friends' substituted. They thanked them for the generous present and added: 'We see you write from a place called Lahore. We have looked in the old school atlas but we can find no such place. But we hope that you are none of you up to any mischief.'

There is a photograph of the Simpson twins, taken in 1865 when Sir Robert visited them in Derry on his return from India; they both wore red wigs and their fingers appear twisted by rheumatism into identical shape. In the nineteen-twenties my father found the old school atlas, which had been printed in 1800 and used at Foyle College by Robert, the Lawrences, McClintocks, and many others, with their names scribbled over it in ink. In its map of India Lahore is plainly marked! But the letter to the Simpson twins with the £200 had omitted 'India' in its address, and the brothers would not have known what continent to look for.

The extent of power and influence exercised by the twenty-four, very wealthy, men who formed the Court of Directors of the Honourable East India Company is not perhaps generally known. When Robert left Foyle College the Company was still the agent through which all British interests and territory in India was administered and controlled. This control covered both political and military service, and the directors had the right to appoint not only civil officers, but also the officers of the Company's Madras, Bengal and Bombay native armies, who did not have to purchase their military commission as British army officers did. Each director had the right to nominate every year, for employment in the Company's service, three assistant surgeons, three civil servants (writers) and twelve military cadets. The writers, and those cadets earmarked for the engineer corps and the artillery, were trained initially in England, the civil servants at the East India College at Haileybury, and the cadets at the Company's Military Seminary at Addiscombe. Candidates for cavalry and infantry regiments normally went direct to India without any preliminary training in England, though occasionally a few selected infantry cadets did go to Addiscombe. All were granted their commission, under the Crown, by the Commander-in-Chief in India.

Robert certainly owed the start of his career to the influence of a Director of the Company. This was Josias Dupré Alexander, a Member of Parliament at Westminster, who happened (perhaps fortunately!) to be a near relative of the Reverend Mounsey Alexander, Robert's stepfather. Mounsey had been Rector of Moville when he married Robert's mother, then Susan McClintock; but Mounsey died young in 1790, and thirteen years later Susan Alexander was married again, to the Reverend Samuel Law Montgomery, and so for the second time became the wife of a Rector of Moville. This complicated development, along with Robert's two marriages and his eight children, my other, (maternal) grandfather, Dean Farrar's ten children, and my parents nine children, has not helped to unravel our family relationships! In this setting Robert began his career in a very unusual way. Josias had nominated Robert for Addiscombe and his nephew William Ferguson Alexander for Haileybury when he discovered, much to his annoyance, that William was a failure and could never be accepted as a civil servant. He therefore contrived successfully to swop the careers of William and Robert, the former going from Haileybury direct to Indian Infantry, and the latter from Addiscombe to the Company's Civil Service. However Robert, having qualified as a military cadet, was actually commissioned in the Bengal Engineers, though he was never a soldier and his name never appeared in any Army List. The official record of William Ferguson Alexander is pathetically short. It simply states that 'Ensign W. F. Alexander joined the 50th Bengal Native Infantry on 11th June 1827. He died of fever on 25th March 1833'.

Clearly patronage had a part in this strange affair, for in 1825 when Robert was still at Addiscombe, Josias Alexander wrote to Susan Montgomery and said, *inter alia*: 'I will smooth Robert's path at Addisco ɔe in preparation for his transfer to the civil line of the Company's service ...' There is also some evidence that at one time

Josias had been on intimate terms with Robert's mother, when the latter, as a young and lovely girl, had been renowned for her beauty in all the counties of Ulster. She was a blonde, very tall with a beautiful figure, and this might conceivably have assisted the exercise of patronage by Josias Alexander in favour of her son at a later stage!

Robert Montgomery's contemporaries at Addiscombe included men who later became very famous, notably Sir Henry Durand and Field-Marshal Lord Napier of Magdala. The former died in India in most unusual circumstances, and no doubt for this reason Robert recorded the event in detail in his papers. Robert was living in London at the time and Sir Henry had been a close friend of his since they were cadets together.

In the winter of 1871, Sir Henry Durand, then Lieutenant-Governor of the Punjab, was on tour in his province and had reached the walled town of Tank in the Derajat, a district between the Indus and the Afghan frontier, overlooked by the arid and rocky foothills of the Suleiman Mountains. Sir Henry was making a ceremonial entry into the township, riding on one of the Lieutenant-Governor's state elephants and accompanied in the howdah by the Nawab of Tank. The latter's son rode in advance with a strong escort of irregular cavalry, whilst behind the Lieutenant-Governor came a second elephant on which rode the Deputy Commissioner of Dera Ismal Khan, the Secretary to the Government of the Punjab, and the Lieutenant-Governor's ADC. A mounted detachment of Punjab police brought up the rear. The whole procession, the cavalry with their swords drawn, the blue and white pennons fluttering from the lances of the police, and the full dress uniforms of the Lieutenant-Governor and his staff, presented a brilliant oriental picture. The town was crowded with tribesmen (Afghans, Pathans, Brahuis and Baluchis), riding or driving their camels, horses and donkeys, all come to witness the arrival of tne Governor Sahib.

At the entrance to Tank there were two gateways, the outer one being of sufficient height to allow any Indian elephant and howdah, with riders, to pass under it; but the inner gateway was lower and at the approach to it the ground rose somewhat. The Lieutenant-Governor's elephant had passed beneath the outer gate with ease, but at the inner gate care would be needed to guide the elephant beneath the archway.

On this occasion the Lieutenant-Governor's elephant, having passed under the outer gate at its proper sedate walk, suddenly increased its pace and ran for the inner entrance, through which the rear file of the cavalry escort had already passed. The mahout tried in vain to control him (he was a full-grown bull elephant standing nearly nine feet tall at the shoulder) but could not do so. Tragedy followed, for the elephant literally charged at the inner gateway, the howdah struck the brickwork of its Mughal arch and broke into pieces, sweeping the Lieutenant-Governor and the Nawab to the ground with all their accoutrements, including the long ceremonial howdah cloth, embossed with gold and silver mountings. The officers on the second elephant immediately got down and found Sir Henry lying face down on the ground unconscious. He died the following morning on New Year's Day.

Many men, and their wives and families, who went to India in the service of the East India Company, met with early or sudden death, due to war, murder, sickness, disease or accident. But the manner of death of Sir Henry Durand, at the summit of his career, was most tragic because the accident could so easily have been avoided.

When my grandfather left Addiscombe he was still only sixteen and too young to begin his service in India. So for the following two years, 'to complete his scholastic education', he went to Wraxall Hall School in North Wiltshire, a large rambling Elizabethan house with an inner courtyard and large gardens. Henry and John Lawrence were there at the same time, for the same reason, but it seems doubtful whether any of them actually improved their education by going there. The only available record of their days at Wraxall emphasised the hardships in winter, when, in the morning, the bedrooms were so cold that water froze hard in the basins and they had to break ice out of their clothing!

2
Writer and Collector

In 1828 young Robert Montgomery, aged just eighteen, arrived in India to begin his duties as a writer in the Bengal Civil Service. He had left Ireland six months earlier and it probably did not then occur to him that he was destined not to return there, except for one period of home furlough, for nearly forty years. He had sailed from Liverpool in an East Indiaman during the first week of June 1828. The vessel in which he made the 15,000 miles voyage to Calcutta, round South Africa, was the *Abberton*, a wooden, three-masted, fully-rigged ship of only 431 tons, chartered by the East India Company mainly for her cargo-carrying capacity. With the passenger accommodation of secondary importance she was built on bluff lines with a maximum speed of under twelve knots and an average daily run of not more than 120 miles.

In those days the risks of shipwreck, fire and piracy were always present. Otherwise, apart from boredom, bad weather, and anguish from seasickness for bad sailors, the major problems for passengers were the inconveniences, particularly the minute cabins, little bigger than cupboards, or no cabins at all of young male passengers like Robert. Privacy did not exist and food deteriorated as the voyage lengthened, particularly meat, as poultry and sheep were kept on deck until all had been eaten, or more likely lost overboard in rough weather. No smoking was ever allowed in a sailing ship, and after dark, reading or writing by passengers was virtually impossible, as the only lighting permitted, from candle lanterns, was strictly limited and controlled. These conditions, generally, did not change until the era of steam ships, and the opening of the Suez Canal in 1869 revolutionised sea travel between Europe and Asia.

In spite of the discomfort, Robert much enjoyed the complete novelty of his long journey to India. He described it all in a letter to his parents dated 10th August, the day on which the *Abberton* had crossed the Equator. But to his dismay the captain, because it was a Sunday, would not allow the crew to carry out the traditional 'crossing the line' visit to the ship by King Neptune; in those days all 'newcomers' to the Equator had to pay half-a-crown for grog for the crew, and those who refused were let down from a yard-arm by a rope into the sea, and ducked three times. Another matter Robert recorded, though not in the letter to his parents, was the highly indecent song sung by the seamen of the crew, generally when pumping out the ship's bilges! The young lady passengers, brought up and chaperoned in the strict fashion of their generation, were not allowed to listen to such sinful behaviour. He had never before sailed the oceans and he spent much time on deck, particularly when nearing the African coastline before sunrise. Then he saw that wonderful scene, the tropic dawn, with the land suddenly climbing out of the darkness and in the far background, against a growing band of light, the peaks of high mountains or forest-clad hills; it was all so new to him, especially the hot weather after the climate of his native Donegal.

Just before my grandfather left home for India his two unmarried sisters, Charlotte Alexander and Mary Susan (the first three years older and the second two years younger than he) cut off a lock of his hair as a keepsake. They adored him and they greatly feared they would never see him again. Growing up in an atmosphere dominated by family ties and mutual devotion, in which sentiment played a large part, this was their way of retaining a contact with him. They placed this lock of hair in a sealed envelope, on which they wrote: 'Lock of hair of our dear Robert, taken May 28th 1828 at 7.30 o'clock in the morning when he left New Park for India'. I have just opened this envelope, the seal of which does not appear to have been broken, and there, lying inside a fold of paper, is a lock of auburn hair, thick and curly, with all its lustre quite untarnished after a century and a half in darkness. I sealed the envelope in haste. His eldest sister also gave him a pocket bible, with a note which so well reveals the rigidity of the religious atmosphere, with its strict morality, in which so many Irish Protestant families of those times were reared, that it is worth quoting:

> May the precepts this blessed book contains be your constant study, my dearest Robert. Always remember it is more painful to repair one fault than avoid a hundred. When perusing its contents, though divided by the wide sea, may you cast a thought on her to whom absence only makes you more dear.

The immediately practical effect a note of this kind will have had on a young man of nineteen, just leaving for a great adventure in a part of the world still largely unknown, is probably not difficult to appreciate. But he also received, again in the custom of his time, one thousand words of parting advice from his father, his reaction to which is included below. I quote only a short extract from the letter:

> Never go in debt, act always with the strictest integrity, be economical but not parsimonius. I strongly recommend you to keep an account of all your expenses and receipts, you have an order with you for more than £200 that I hope will be sufficent to set you up. If however any difficulty should arise, draw on me for £100 and Mr Alexander [brother of Mounsey Alexander] will cash it.

In the event this sound advice was difficult to follow because Robert became very much in debt! In his time the Company's officers, civil and military, were never well, or even sufficiently, paid and no doubt for this reason he recorded in his papers:

> From the day I first landed in Calcutta I was always in debt, and remained so for the next thirty years until I became Lieutenant-Governor of a province.

Robert got his first sight of India, which somewhat disappointed him, from the deck of *Abberton* as she sailed up the Hooghli river during the last eighty-five miles of the long voyage to Calcutta. The banks were low and muddy, and there was little to see on either shore except apparently endless mangrove swamps or dense jungle with dwarf trees. When night fell the ship was moored to the river bank and, attempting to sleep on deck, he spent the first of many exhausting nights in tropical India; of course he was heavily attacked by mosquitoes and lay awake listening to the sounds of jackal hunting in packs, to the weird howl of hyenas, and sometimes the blood-curdling whine of tigers on their prowl for game.

However, as his ship neared Calcutta the scene changed completely. The Kidderpore docks had not yet been built, but downstream from the city along the so-called Garden Reach, and for eleven miles upstream as far as Barrackpore, large residences could be seen; for the British had begun to build for themselves English-style country houses with pleasant green lawns sloping down to the river bank.

At this time Calcutta already had a population of just under 190,000, and was growing rapidly as the commercial capital for the rich trade of the East India Company. Great industries like iron, jute, coal, tea, rice, vegetable oils, textiles and timber, were already well established; furthermore the whole internal trade of the Company was about to expand enormously with the coming of railways and river steamers. Calcutta was also the seat of the Governor-General, then Lord William Cavendish-Bentinck, and the headquarters of the Commander-in-Chief of the Army in India. It was just over ten years since the war that had finally ended

Maratha power in the subcontinent, and the Mughal Empire was already defunct in real terms. All Bengal was under British rule, which in the north west extended as far as the Sutlej River. In the south, Mysore had been subdued and the Emperor's Viceroy, the Nizam of Hyderabad, only retained his position through British support. Virtually in all India only the Sikh Kingdom of Ranjit Singh, in the Punjab, still remained outside the sphere of British influence. This, broadly, was the state of affairs in India when Robert Montgomery disembarked at Calcutta on 13th November 1828.

The city was already, in outline, beginning to take the shape it had assumed by the time of Independence. The Maidan was there, with its enormous Government House built some twenty years earlier, but there was no huge Anglican cathedral at one end, nor of course the imposing statue of the Queen Empress Victoria at the other end; and no Dalhousie Square, as we knew it, with its large banks, big commercial houses and smart shops.

To young Robert, standing on the Maidan and facing east towards Chowringhee, which was eventually to become the 'Oxford Street' of Calcutta, it was the great variety of people, animals and transport, moving in a constant flow day and night, that chiefly impressed him. At first he was amazed to see people conveyed in rickshaws drawn by coal-black natives, or in palanquins carried by two men, with heavily curtained windows for women and young girls in purdah; for a lady of birth must never be seen by a stranger, though sometimes one caught sight of a girl's face peeping shyly through a chink in a curtain. He also noticed that everyone dressed according to his or her religion, caste, race or profession, with no regard whatever for fashion as he knew it; women always wore the sari, probably dirty, brown and ragged unless they were people of standing, and he soon appreciated the distinction between the Hindu in his dhoti and the Muslim wearing trousers. He soon ceased to be surprised at the sight of completely naked men in the streets, carrying huge bundles on their heads, or of a *sadhu* (holy man) clad in nothing but a paste of cow-dung and ashes daubed over his head and body; or of a lone cow straying, unattended, across a road with no one attempting to control it.

Very soon after his arrival Robert discovered, at the far end of Chowringhee, the region which was later to become the centre of European social life in Calcutta, and which in his day was beginning to assume that role, being known as the residential quarter of the British official and commercial population. As yet no wealthy Indians lived there. Here there were large imposing houses, some with gravel entrance drives, and all with lawns and gardens bright with flower beds and varied, coloured shrubs. Servants, clad in long red or white tunics with wide coloured belts and turbans, could be seen about their business, whilst ayahs sat in the shade of big trees tending the young children of their

10

masters. It was the scene in which he himself was to live for many years, and which continued into our time - maybe it will for all time.

All newly-joined civil servants, on arrival in Calcutta, went first to the Training College at Fort William in order, particularly, to complete their learning of the Company's languages; these were Hindi, Urdu, Persian, Arabic, Bengali and Sanskrit. The standard was extremely high with a very stiff examination after a one year course, at the end of which the Governor-General presided at a 'Public Disputation' and issued the Pass Certificates; any new entrant who failed was 'debarred from employment in the Company's service', and very few did fail. Military officers were not allowed to attend these courses without a special application from the Adjutant-General, which was seldom made. The average linguistic standard in the Bengal Civil Service was therefore always far higher than that in the in Bengal Army, with the exception of Engineer and Artillery officers whose course at Addiscombe had included a thorough grounding in the Company's languages. This complete lack of organised language instruction for young cavalry and infantry officers, before joining their regiments, must have contributed substantially to the overall causes of the Indian Mutiny. A training college for them was set up at Baraset in Calcutta, but it did not last long, unfortunately, and was closed down in 1821.

Perhaps the most damning indictment of the system lies in the quality of the Company's advice, given to their cadets (many still only seventeen years old) before they sailed from the United Kingdom for India. Extracts like the following[3] appear ludicrous today:

Languages Urdu: colloquial proficiency can be acquired in a few weeks. Four months study with a *munshi* [teacher] should be enough to qualify for an interpretership.

The climate and nature of military duties admit of abundant leisure. For nearly 12 hours a day, for most of the year, an officer can be a prisoner in his own house.

Not exactly a pleasant outlook for a young cadet joining the Company's army! Leave to the UK was allowed only once during his whole service in India, and never before ten years had been spent there.

Having been trained at Addiscombe, Robert had no difficulty in passing his Fort William course, and therefore found ample time to enjoy the distractions of Calcutta social life which were so readily available. Evidently there was soon a need to spend that £200, given him by his father in the 'hope it will be sufficient to set you up'! Small wonder when one considers the situation of an inexperienced Irish youth of just nineteen, suddenly pitched into Calcutta society with all its brilliance and

11

excitement, early morning and evening rides over the Maidan, the races, picnics, dances and dinner parties. In this he was very different from John Lawrence, who, though always his great friend, avoided all forms of social life as far as he possibly could and cared nothing for appearances. Just before he left Fort William, Robert wrote a letter to his two aunts, Sally and Mary Montgomery (his father's sisters) in which he tells them something of life in Bengal over a hundred and fifty years ago. The two sisters never married and lived then at 13 London Street, Londonderry.

Monday 30 November 1829

My dear Aunts,
I cannot think of letting so favourable an opportunity pass, as the sailing of *Roxborough Castle*, the fastest sailor we have, without writing a few lines to let you know how I am. Two Derry men called on me yesterday, one of them, Ross McClintock, is an Assistant Surgeon on board *Princess Charlotte*, and the other Helen Harvey's nephew. In fact since I came to India I have seen a great number of Derry people. I hear that Mr Grant's son is getting on uncommonly well, and has I believe 300 rupees a month, so that with a little care he may live extremely comfortably. There is much grandeur and magnificence here and everything that can be desired, except the presence of kind friends at London Street. Is Catherine Murray married yet, or does she still show her beautiful face at the window as formerly? I hope on 16th December to be out of this Fort William when I am almost sure of being appointed to Mr Gouldsbury, Collector at Dinapore. There is beautiful hog hunting near there with abundance of tigers, bears, and all those ferocious sort of animals, but you need not be at all alarmed as I shall be mounted on an elephant when I may fire at them at pleasure and they will not be able to get at me. The hogs are the most dangerous as you are obliged to charge at them on horseback with a spear in your hand and they always charge at you, so if by any chance you tumble off, it is all over with you, as their tusks are somewhat longer than 4 inches. Frederick and Uncle McClintock who are now sitting at table with me desire to be remembered to you, and I send you my love, particularly your Derry friends and all at New Park.

Believe me to remain
ever your affectionate nephew
R. Montgomery

Pigsticking is not referred to again in Robert's papers, and it seems likely he gave it up on leaving Calcutta; certainly he never achieved the niceties of technique practised by experts, who varied the length of the spear used, and the way it was carried, to suit changes in the nature and level of the ground ridden over. He also apparently gave up tiger shooting in the jungle from an elephant howdah or a *machan* (a platform built in the tree tops) - a relatively safe sport compared with the dangerous pursuit of hunting tiger on foot. My grandfather and some of his friends also kept

12

a scratch pack of hounds, of mixed breeds, with which they hunted jackal on the west bank of the Hooghli. After a kill they were in the habit of throwing jackal bones to the evil-looking vultures perched in nearby trees, which fed on garbage. However, the young men had put gun powder and a slow match in the bones, so when the vultures pounced on them, with their long hooked beaks and sharp claws, the effect may be imagined! No doubt an exceedingly cruel practice, though the vulture has always been regarded as vermin fit only for destruction. Nevertheless it has to be said that some thirty years later some of these same young officers were just as cruel to sepoys of the Bengal Army who were convicted of mutiny and murder.

Robert left Calcutta in December 1829 on his appointment, not to Dinapore on the Ganges as he had expected, but to Azamgarh in the North Western Provinces. At that time these Provinces covered a vast area of the Indo-Gangetic plain stretching from Benares in the east as far as the Sutlej River in the north west. In between were great and important cities like Allahabad, Cawnpore, Lucknow, Agra, Meerut and of course Delhi, still the seat of the Great Mughal who was, in name only, the Emperor of all Hindustan. The northern limit of this huge province lay in the foothills of the immense Himalayan mountain range, with its southern border formed by the forests and hills of Central India and Bihar, and extending in the west as far as the state of Indore. Paradoxically the King of Oudh, the chief Muslim ruler of northern India, not yet under British rule, remained in the very centre of the Ganges Valley, a feudal lord scarcely paying lip service to his Emperor at Delhi. The district of Azamgarh was about a hundred miles north of Benares in the region which later became the United Provinces of Agra and Oudh. Robert was to be Assistant to the joint Magistrate, Collector[4] and Settlement Officer, Mr James Thomason, a development which he later recognised could not have been more opportune, for he was brought under the influence of a most remarkable and influential man.

James Thomason was a product of Haileybury who became one of the great Indian administrators of the nineteenth century, and was highly regarded for his professional knowledge and efficiency at all levels of government. His father, a chaplain in the Bengal Ecclesiastical Service, was fervently religious; so much so that when once shipwrecked and nearly drowned with all his family (including young James) off the coast of Burma, he was able 'to rejoice in God's will that had brought them such measure of disaster'. Brought up in this atmosphere, James Thomason became a fanatical churchman, and an enthusiastic member of the Evangelical party, which, in the first half of the last century had a marked effect on British religious and social life. Those who belonged to that school of thought believed it was incumbent on them at all times to 'improve the occasion', deeming it unfaithful to be reticent, in speech and

13

writing, about religious or sacred matters. This belief stands out very clearly in Thomason's many letters to Robert, including his conviction that it was God's purpose and will to place India under British protection and rule.

But Thomason was not only a high grade administrator. He was also an expert instructor, second to none in his ability to train young men such as Robert, in their task of 'settlement'. Very briefly 'settlement' meant finding solutions for the many complex legal, financial, economic and social problems, which the Company's civil servants had to face, following the collapse of the Muslim administration of the Mughal Empire. In the forefront of all these problems was the legal ownership of land and property, the relationship between landlords and their tenants, and (perhaps the most difficult of all) the assessment and collection of land revenue taxes; finally, surmounting all else, there was the immense problem of maintaining law and order, generally with the need to raise a new police force in the first place.

I have written at length about James Thomason's character for three reasons. First, because of the massive influence he exerted on so many of his young subordinates, and therefore on events during the critical years before 1857; secondly because Thomason was not without his critics – one modern historian has even gone so far as to say that his policies led in part to the outbreak of the mutiny in the Bengal Army[5] – and finally because Robert Montgomery was soon to marry James Thomason's younger sister, though, as will be seen, my grandfather never came entirely under the sway of his first, most famous, employer.

Robert spent more than seven years at Azamgarh, much of the time under the direct authority of James Thomason; the latter always delegated considerable power and authority to his assistants and then held them responsible for results, so that men liked working for him. For Robert it was a period of learning, training and experience, with the last three years as the officially appointed Joint Magistrate, Collector and Settlement Officer. The district was a large and populous one, with an area of some 2,500 square miles, within which lived more than one million six hundred thousand people. It was part of the old Hindustan, so called by the Muslim conquerors of the early Hindus, the centuries-old India of the villages located in the upper basins of three great rivers – the mighty Ganges, Jumna and Gogra – with, as a result, a soil of unrivalled fertility, though still subject to all the horrors of famine when the monsoons failed. The country people were mainly peasant farmers from two orthodox Hindu castes of Brahmans and Rajputs, in their various subdivisions, so many of whom were recruited into and indeed formed the greater part of the old Bengal Native Army.

In the eighteen-thirties the white population in provincial India was still very small. In the whole of Bengal, apart from Calcutta city, there were less than 300 adult white women with some 4000 males, virtually all of them British army officers and their families, or British officers of the civil administration. When Robert arrived in Azamgarh the only other white residents at the station were the Collector (Thomason), his wife, and an assistant surgeon; a total of four with himself. The sudden contrast socially with life in Calcutta must have depressed him, for he described it in the following terms:[6]

> Azamgarh is a small detached station, separated from all civilisation as if it had just been dropped in the middle of the jungle. It has a desolate appearance with no roads or bridges, only three public buildings, including the Court house, in a corner of which I live, and just two private houses. There is no Church, nor as yet any school building, and the nearest civilian residents are at Jaunpore 60 miles away; we are thus isolated.

In 1830 communications, up-country, were still the main problem, for there were as yet no railways, and virtually no roads, only tracks. Steam boats for river navigation were only just beginning. Main highways like the Grand Trunk Road from Calcutta to Peshawar were not begun until 1833, and it was James Thomason who was responsible for that road's initial construction. Journeys were always made on horseback or in a 'buggy' (a light two-wheeled gig also called a *tum-tum*), whilst long-distance passengers with heavy baggage went by *dak gari*. The latter was a slow, very uncomfortable and tiring version of horse-drawn public transport which moved in short stages, generally at night, to avoid the great heat of the day. The *dak* was particularly unpopular on account of its dangers, for the country swarmed with robbers and armed men, including gangs of thugs (the anglicised version of the Hindu word *thagi* who strangled their victims).

My grandfather's papers at this time make no mention at all of the army, or of any military matter, though even in a very small station there was generally a garrison, because a wide distribution of troops was considered essential for internal security. But at Azamgarh there was no garrison until early in 1834, when Ensign Phayre (later General Sir Arthur Phayre, GCMG, KCSI, CB) arrived from Gorakhpore with a small detachment (probably at platoon strength) of his regiment, the 7th Bengal Native Infantry. However Robert did not refer to this new arrival, even though one more white face in such a small community must have contributed to the station's very limited amenities.

The Indo-subcontinent is a land of colour and sunshine where, broadly speaking, there is no real winter climate except in the foothills and mountains of the Himalaya ('Abode of Snow'). In the wide alluvial valley of the Ganges the best months are from October to February, when the days are pleasantly warm and the nights relatively cold; then the temperature rises rapidly and by early March the hot weather of the great tropical plain has begun, with shade temperatures sometimes reaching 118° Fahrenheit. However, in those far off times the British did not go to the hills to escape the great heat; there was nowhere to go, for hill stations generally, as we knew them, were not begun much before the eighteen-forties and it never occurred to my grandfather and his contemporaries, in their early days, to leave the plains and find relief in a cooler atmosphere. They never knew the joy (as we did) of the long drive or ride along a road that climbed to the mountains, snaking round hills, twisting, winding and often bending back on itself; whilst every moment the air got cooler as you passed through the pine forests, intermingled with ilex, cedar and elm. Then you saw, apparently quite near, the high snow-covered peaks, range after range of them, gleaming like ice pinnacles as they soared into space and disappeared.

At Azamgarh the worst part was the humidity, for the level of perspiration and resultant prickly heat was terrible, especially for the women. Crinolines did not reach India until the Mutiny, and the women were always completely clothed from neckline to ankle in dresses of grey or dark material and always with long sleeves. Not surprisingly therefore, settlement officers like my grandfather preferred to do their touring as far as possible during the cooler months. This part of the valley country had a quiet beauty of its own, with great unending fields of sugar cane, rice, cotton, indigo (then a very important industry before synthetic dyes appeared), millet and maize. Rice and pulses, chiefly peas, beans and lentils, formed the staple diet of the people and were cultivated profusely. Every three miles or so there was a village with the huts roofed in brown palm leaf thatch (the corrugated iron roof was unknown in those days), and built always in the shade of mango or pipal trees, the latter with their branches leaning over and rooted into the ground. Vegetable and garden crops were always a feature of every village, poppies, peppers, mint, fennel, with masses of trailing tomatoes and cucumbers growing all over the thatch, and of course banana groves.

This was the country through which Robert rode, on horseback or on an elephant, with his baggage loaded on camels or in ox-carts. He had so much to learn, including the need for discretion in relying, or not, as the case might be, on the advice of his native clerk. He had to survey each property in every village, measure its extent, establish its legal ownership between several claimants, including the buildings and water supply, and assess the whole for revenue tax; all this in a country where the population was 86 per cent Hindu, though the landlords were generally Muslims, descendants of the Mughal conquerors. Then a canal had to be planned, a bridge site chosen, or a new school building inspected. In short a whole framework of civil administration had to be provided, and the young district officer of those days was the only authority who could sanction, amend or refuse any local plan or proposal. He rode all day, with an armed police escort, until the tents were pitched about tea-time, after which, as magistrate he must sit in court, probably under a green mango tree, hear cases (applicants, complaints, prosecutions) and administer justice.

When my grandfather had completed four years at Azamgarh, James Thomason's sister, Frances Mary (she was always called Fanny) arrived from England to live with her brother and his wife. She was seventeen years old, a simple and retiring girl, who had led a very sheltered life, wholly given to duty. She was also deeply religious, with a firm belief in all the tenets of the Evangelical party, and the shock she experienced on her arrival was immense. She could not possibly have foreseen the isolation and, to her, the completely new physical conditions of life that awaited her at Azamgarh. She was a slim girl, a brunette and very attractive in a demure way, with her hair always parted in the middle over a broad forehead and drawn down covering the ears, to be tied back with a bow at the nape of the neck; she had a full mouth and a firm chin with an expression suggesting a high degree of composure - which she certainly needed in all the circumstances of her life in India. Robert was the only bachelor Fanny Thomason ever met at Azamgarh, or would have been allowed to meet, for James Thomason, and she also, would not have looked on young Ensign Phayre as a suitable friend for any young teenage girl!

Not long after Fanny arrived she began to accompany Robert on one-day tours from Azamgarh, either riding with him or driving in a buggy, but she was never allowed to remain in camp with him overnight; the conventions of their generation were very strict and to disregard them was unthinkable. Some of the letters he sent back to her, before they became engaged, show how the servant problems in his time were very similar to those we experienced in India in our day. He seldom dated any of his letters:

Camp Mhow

I arrived here very early this morning, I mean about 8 o'clock, which considering that I had 18 miles of road to go over was pretty well. I breakfasted immediately on my arrival, and have been hard at work ever since, I mean till I could see no longer. The Bearer will be fined two annas for forgetting to bring any soap. I have not even a piece wherewith to wash my hands!

Another letter followed in similar vein:

I lost my temper badly today with my bearer and I think I had provocation. I told him to awaken me an hour before day break. He did not: to have hot

17

water ready for my tea before I started: he did not: he had sent ahead my *solar topee* and my map. This I could not stand and I pitched into him properly.

Early in November 1834 Fanny Thomason accompanied her brother James and Mary his wife on an extensive tour of the district. Robert was with them and they were still on tour five weeks later. She began to keep a diary on 7th November in which she wrote every day for the rest of her life. Evidently they got engaged on 2nd December during the day's march, on horseback, to the next camp, for her diary entry for that day reads:

An eventful day the events of which are too deeply graven on my mind to need anything to remind me of it. It was a long ride, my first time with 'him', and I drove in the buggy the rest of the march; took a walk in the evening and lost our way ...' Robert galloped off to find the buggy.

On 4th December she sent a very long letter to her half-sister Eliza Hutchinson in which she wrote, *inter alia*:

Camp Chiriakote

My very dearest Eliza,
   Brother James' letter has reached you ere this, what *did* you say on reading it? I would have given anything to have seen you without being seen myself at the moment that you opened it. Were you surprised? Perhaps you were for I am sure I never gave the slightest hint of my feelings but, on the contrary, I rather think that if I have ever mentioned him to whom I have now *given* my heart it has been in terms which would lead you to conclude anything but what was really the case. Mary even could not discover what my sentiments were, and two or three times she has tried to sound me, but I was quite aware of what she was doing and never once was off my guard. The fact was feelings had got possession of my mind, which it would have been impossible to define; they were such as I certainly never experienced before, and I could not allow *myself* to believe what I felt; but what is the use of my endeavouring to describe to you what I could not understand myself. You have been in the same situation and will far better imagine than I can describe. All I know, dear Eliza, is that I am *very very* happy!! Who would have thought a few months ago that such a change would have taken place. Love is mystery indeed, how insensibly it works. What would I give, my own dear sister, if you could be with me on the *happy* day that is to unite me for life to my dear Robert.
   Oh! Eliza, you will love him, I know you will for my sake. What adds to my happiness in no small degree is to see how happy dear James and Mary are, and you too dear. I feel sure you will be glad to hear of the choice I have made. He is not a stranger to you. *The* day has just been fixed for the 17th of this month. Rather quick work you will say, but why should it be delayed? Mr and Mrs Tucker are to come from Azamgarh to Mahomedabad where the ceremony will be performed by the Reverend Mr Pratt in a tent (romantic is it

not?). We then proceed to Mhow for the honeymoon. And now, my very dearest Eliza, what shall I say more? This letter has occupied me the whole day, and thoughts cannot always be controlled. Judge where mine are ...

Certainly fourteen days seems a very short engagement but this young couple, he was twenty-five and she seventeen, very much wanted to become husband and wife. Getting the marriage license and arranging for a chaplain to marry them were difficult matters, which took Robert away from Azamgarh for three days; but Mr Pratt (the chaplains were always touring) would be at Mahomedabad in Ghazipore district, seventy miles from Azamgarh, on 17th December. Finally there could be no question of a trousseau for Fanny as there were no European shops worthy of the name nearer than Calcutta, and one week before the wedding she entered in her diary: 'December 11th. Received some things from Calcutta; a hat, gloves, and some lace.'

So the marriage took place as planned, very simply in a tent with no choir and no music except human voices. The only wedding guests were James Thomason with his wife and Henry Carre Tucker (another district officer and very close friend) and his wife. But there was a small congregation of local men and women, converts to Christianity, and they all sang hymns with great gusto and were very happy. Life was tough in those days for the young district officers and their wives, as Fanny Montgomery soon came to know.

Not long after Robert's marriage, James Thomason left Azamgarh to become Secretary to the Government of the North-Western Provinces under Sir Charles Metcalfe. My grandfather succeeded Thomason as Collector of Azamgarh District and he and Fanny were able to make their first home in the Thomason's house. However, to her dismay, Fanny Montgomery now became very lonely as her husband was so often away in camp; after her marriage she seldom accompanied him on tour and certainly took no part at all in his work, and she missed her brother and his wife. In her case this was particularly unfortunate, as she made no attempt to learn Urdu or Bengali and had nothing to fall back on except her own resources, which were wholly domestic and maternal. To keep herself occupied she wrote daily in her diary of even the smallest event, and then copied out extracts from commentaries and sermons, with verses from hymns and devotional poems. The result was pathetic but expressed so well her innocence and simplicity as well as her great love for her husband. My father destroyed all his step-mother's writings, including her diary, retaining only one letter she wrote to Robert and two of her pencil drawings; in the Bishop's view the generations that followed would not be interested in the personal record of a young woman whose nature was so unselfish and dutiful. Of course her circumstances were not made easier by the birth of her children. The first, a daughter, was born in October

19

1835, then a son in December the following year, and another daughter two years later; finally a still-born child in 1840, and another still-born birth two years afterwards. Truly a tragic record for under eight years of married life during which her physical life must have been conditioned, virtually each year, by childbearing or miscarriage. She and Robert fervently believed that children came from God, and never by family planning or control. Her only surviving letter to her husband, written not long after the birth of her first child, speaks for itself:

Asamgarh 21st March 1836

My beloved Robert,
 To think that I am not to see you again for a whole week seems dreadful to me, and when I awoke this morning and found you gone, the fact of your having been with me, even for a day, appeared a dream. I could scarcely believe I had seen you at all. After breakfast they came to ask me where the door in the bathing room wall was to be made, and as I despaired of making myself understood, we were not able to explain. The mistri [carpenter] said he could complete your bathing room in four days. Did Mr Campbell tell you, dear, that the chintz was to cost 99 rupees because here is Mr Taylor's letter in which he says 94. I ought to have too the letter about the painter. Musa (a bearer) I think has the box (a black and green one) into which I put a number of letters, and when I get that I will send you them all that you may see and make out the accounts, and what the painter is to receive.
 I long to hear from you, dearest Robert, but will not expect to do so till the day after tomorrow.
 Well, my own dearest one, goodbye for today. I am just going to bathe our little Treasure.

Ever with tenderest love
Your own Fan

 Looking back it is not difficult to recognise Fanny's plight, for the dreadful boredom she suffered was certainly shared, in equal or lesser degree, by successive generations of British women in India. At Azamgarh she had virtually no one she could talk to, no station library and no newspapers, no gymkhana club with tennis courts and swimming pool, not even croquet (that came to India later and was first played on earth or gravel with very heavy mallets and croquet balls and hoops up to eight inches wide); worst of all for Fanny there was no church, and memsahibs were not expected to take part in household duties as there was never any lack of servants. Finally the health problems for any young married couple of the Company's Civil Service of those days, serving up-country, made life very difficult; the young assistant surgeon at Azamgarh was seldom there, and self-treatment was generally their only remedy, so much so that it was accepted as part of their daily life. Some of Robert's letters to Fanny describe what happened:

20

In Camp
[No date given]

Dearest Fan

A man here has been seized with cholera and the people have asked me for some medicine. Pray, dear, drop 40 drops of laudanum into a small wine glass full of brandy and send it to me. Don't be afraid if there are half a dozen drops too much.

You are the best wife that ever lived. It is only since I married you that my expenses have been so small. I send you 180 rupees. When I return pray have dinner on the table exactly at 5 o'clock.

A district officer on tour had to be all things to all men including doctor when necessary. The concoction Fanny had to send her husband (laudanum is a tincture of opium) was thought to afford some relief from cholera. In those days 180 rupees would be regarded as a quite substantial sum. Robert's mind was evidently turning with relish to a change from his camp meals!

Another letter from Robert to his wife is equally relevant:

In Camp

My dearest Fan

It is highly fortunate a doctor is near here. I have become ill with erysipelas in my right leg. The doctor applied 48 leeches to the affected part, upon which I fainted. Two days afterwards he applied 28 more leeches, on which I fainted again. But it is better now.

Here is 30 rupees for my worthy Fan from her unworthy

Hubby

The doctor's treatment appears to have been successful, for the time being at any rate. When he was back at Azamgarh, Robert also recorded:

I was told today to get and administer 20 drops of calomel to my dear Fan. Her mouth and throat have been sore for a month

Apparently, in the absence of a doctor, their only acceptable diet when ill was 'toast and water', no matter what the ailment was and however unappetising it might seem!

The last letter Robert sent to Fanny from camp, before they left Azamgarh, shows both the serious and light-hearted sides of his character. It was a Sunday and he was evidently close to another station head-quarters:

This has been a quiet day, and I hope I may add, a profitable one. You can hardly fancy the stillness there reigns throughout a camp when one is alone;

21

not a sound to be heard, and it seems as if Hindu and Musulman, as well as Christian English, agreed to honour the Sabbath. I had given orders no one was to come to me. I felt the presence of God was very near, and I thought much of you and our dear little ones.

Then abruptly his mood changed and he wrote:

I went into the station last evening (Saturday) and dined with the Cartwright's. I don't know that you would have liked such a laughing set, they never ceased the whole time. They made me sit down to a round game of cards, to which I had no objection as there was a great deal of fun.

Today I have fined the gwala [Hindu cowherd] one rupee, and the tandel [tent-pitcher] another; the former because he will keep the cream and takes all the milk (12 seers) to make butter of daily – he bags 9/10 and I hardly even touch it! The latter because my tent was not yet pitched when I came into camp. I have been looking into accounts and find the bawarchi [the cook] is charging 3½ rupees for feeding turkeys alone! I told him to wring off all their heads. I hope to be able to send you 50 rupees on the 4th. No more at present from your own

R. Montgomery

The need in India to supervise your servant's accounts will not surprise anyone, and 12 seers is 24 lbs weight which seems enough milk for butter every day! During most tours, a day's march on horseback with villages to survey and inspect, covered up to twelve miles. The baggage, on camels or in ox-carts, always went ahead and the Collector would certainly expect to find his tents pitched in some shady mango grove, the horses and camels (with maybe an elephant or two) tethered a suitable distance away, whilst the servants were busy preparing the Collector's dinner.

Robert Montgomery now had over seven years' experience as a district officer up-country. His practical work as a Collector and Settlement Officer was apparently appreciated for he received the following testimony from Sir Frederick Currie, Commissioner of the Gorakhpore Division. The letter is formal and pompous, and shows that no increase in salary, however small, could be approved without reference to the Board of Revenue in Allahabad:

Mr Montgomery's proceedings are entirely approved, and the success with which he has engaged the Land owners to apportion the assessment amongst themselves, and also to dispose of other questions of Settlement, easily adjusted because well understood by themselves, is very satisfactory and highly creditable to that Officer.

Under the circumstances stated by the Board and in consideration of the high opinion which the Lieutenant-Governor entertains of Mr Montgomery's merits, he authorises him to draw a personal allowance so that his whole

22

receipt for any month shall not exceed Rupees 1000, the salary of a Deputy Collector's rank

Shortly after he received this report Robert was informed of his appointment as Collector and Magistrate of the important city and district of Allahabad.

3
City of God

Robert and Fanny Montgomery and their two young children, Frances Mary aged one and a half years and Robert Thomason just five months old, arrived in Allahabad in April 1837. It was a very great change for them; after seven years in a small up-country station they came straight to a busy and growing city, with a population of 70,000 and factories and mills on a scale exceeded only at Calcutta. The great Akbar, most famous of the Mughal conquerors, had restored the military and strategic importance of Allahabad to what it was in the heroic age of the Hindu Empires. It was he who built the magnificent fort, rivalling those at Agra and Delhi, at the very apex of the river junction where the Ganges pours into the Jumna, to continue as one vast stream on its long journey to the delta in the Bay of Bengal. Prag had been the name of the old Hindu city; but Akbar, who wanted Hindu support and appointed many Hindu Rajputs to be his chief officers, had wisely renamed the town Allahabad ('City of God'). It had always been a place of great religious significance equalling Hardwar and Benares (a pillar of the Hindu Emperor Asoka, c. 240 BC, stands within the fort), and to this day millions of pilgrims come annually to bathe at the river confluence. The greatest testimony to this city, in our day, is the fact that on 12th February 1948 the ashes of the Mahatma (Saint and Wise One) Mohandas Karamchand Gandhi were immersed in the holy waters beneath the fortress.

The Collector and Magistrate of a large city and district such as Allahabad, was always a person of some standing and importance; locally he wielded considerable power and influence and it was natural that his residence should match his status. In those days the Civil Lines and the military cantonment were both north of the city proper, the latter being spread out along the left bank of the Jumna with its eastern exit overlooked by the great fortress. The Collector's residence was not far from the lines of the 6th Bengal Native Infantry (the permanent garrison of Allahabad) and was an old 'Company' house, not a bungalow. It was brick-built with one storey above ground level and a flat roof and verandah at the front and on each side; as always the kitchens and servants' quarters were quite separate at the rear. It was an imposing residence but inside it was difficult to keep cool, for it was not until about the end of the eighteen-forties that the British began to appreciate the coolness of ground floor accommodation, and the 'bungalow' came into its own. Until then you either lived in a 'pukka house' (like Robert's at Allahabad) or in a one-storey building with a thatched roof, which was obviously cooler but not quite so prestigious as a 'pukka house'! However the Montgomery's home did face north, which was just as well for Allahabad had long been known as the 'oven of India' on account of its appalling heat and the level of humidity. In the India Office Library there is a map, undated, of the 'Old Civil Lines' at Allahabad which shows prominently a large space of open ground marked 'Ice-pits'. It was still many years before ice factories were constructed in India, but for generations our forbears had been making ice by an ingenious method, and storing it for use in the hot weather.

Allahabad then had two very wide and deep ice-pits, each with well lined and revetted sides and covered with a frame, or lid, of exceptionally thick thatch; a round mud brick house with low walls and a strong thatch roof was erected over each pit. Every evening when the winter frosts began, and this would not be until December, shallow earthenware saucers were laid in rows outside the pits and filled with water, which froze during the night. Early next morning, before dawn, convicts from the Jail (under escort) went round with baskets, collected the ice from the saucers, generally not less than one and a half inches thick from each, and emptied the contents into the pits; the ice was rammed down very hard before each pit was covered with its thatch lid, and the mud houses locked. The next evening the whole process was begun again, and repeated daily in the same way. When the frosts ended early in February the pits were covered over and sealed and not opened again until the 'punkahs' were started in April or May. In my grandfather's papers the entry 'Ice-pits opened today' appears regularly every year; it was clearly an important date, to be looked forward to with pleasure, for ice was a luxury to be used thriftily and with care. The ration per family, always on payment, was about 5 lbs per day and might hopefully be expected to last until mid-August.

Fanny Montgomery had been longing for their transfer to Allahabad for she knew it would mean the end of her loneliness at Azamgarh. Although her husband's working hours in his new post were very long, he was seldom away on tour and she had plenty of friends and acquaintances; above all, for her, there was an Anglican church with a resident chaplain.

In the hot weather, going to church meant rising at 5 a.m., as the usual hour for service was 5.30 in order to avoid the great heat of the day, but that did not deter Fanny from her regular attendance. River steamers were beginning to operate on the Ganges and once a month a ship was due to arrive from Calcutta, from where the 800-mile voyage up-river took at least three weeks. This was always a great event for the station and contributed a lot to its social life which had become very gay and colourful, particularly during the cool months. There were dances and dinner parties (one winter there were no less than fourteen unmarried girls in the station!), a racecourse had been built and the British officers of the garrison were hunting jackal on the north shore of the Ganges, with foxhounds imported from England; a local book society had been started and there were even five or six billiard tables in the larger houses. All these activities grew and developed round a very popular social event referred to in those days as 'Band'. In every station the British community liked to foregather after their evening ride or drive to listen to the local regimental band and to gossip or discuss affairs; of course all this was the forerunner of the station gymkhana club.

Regrettably, I think, there is scant mention of sports and pastimes at Allahabad in my grandfather's papers, except for the game bird shooting which he clearly liked very much. There were over 800 square miles of the Doab (the land between the Ganges and Jumna), still largely jungle and not yet urbanised, in which quail, snipe, grey partridge, wild duck, teal, and hares were very plentiful. But Fanny took no part in any of the station's social or sporting activities, and did not join in its intellectual or cultural life (such as it was), and this, as she was the wife of the Collector, must have been unfortunate for Robert. He summed up his wife in admirable terms when he wrote of her:

she was not formed to shine in the assemblies of the gay, in which her soul did not delight. But she had what was far more estimable, the ornament of a meek and quiet spirit, and for these qualities she was beloved by all who knew her.

It would have been appropriate, I think, if Robert had added how often Fanny's life was clouded by sickness. She suffered much from bouts of enteric fever, and less than a year after her arrival in Allahabad she found she was pregnant again. It seems her happiest hours (when not with her husband) were spent in a long chair on the verandah from where she could look down on their large garden, generally after Robert had left for his office early in the morning, and again awaiting his return in the evening. In the front of the house there was a big lawn, bordered by neam trees and bright with flowers, particularly the scarlet and white hibiscus, poinsettia and many coloured cannas; geraniums grew in profusion, and their privacy was ensured by tall clumps of the beautiful oleander shrub with its fine red, white, and pink flowers, both single and double blossoms. Her greatest joy were the glorious flame trees at the entrance gates, when they flowered in spring.

At this time Fanny did not sleep well (though nothing ever seemed to disturb Robert) and she was generally awake an hour before dawn, when there was light enough in the sky to put out the stars and she could feel the 'dawn wind'; it began as a murmur among the leaves and then brought a cool breath of air through the mesh of her mosquito netting – so refreshing after a night with little relief from perspiration and prickly heat. In her day the memsahibs, especially young girls, did not sleep on camp beds in the garden as we always did in the hot weather. As dawn broke she used to go out on the verandah where she could watch the *malis* (gardeners) already at work watering the lawns and flower beds, without apparently disturbing the bird and animal life around them. Grey squirrels with three white stripes on their back were in the trees, as well as those small insect-eating lizards which she also found in the house; then a toucan, with his large gaily coloured bill, would appear with fruit in his mouth, but he took no notice of the hoopoes strutting round him on the grass. Doves too were everywhere, poking out their heads one way and another, or walking solemnly along a horizontal tree branch, whilst green pigeons, with their lovely soft green plumage and bright red claws, perched in the tree tops. Sometimes she saw a small bird with a breast black above and white below, his tail held high and with a pert blackbird manner. Robert told her it was an ouzel.

Then suddenly it became hot, bird noise ceased and she went inside, to meet maybe a mongoose with his grey fur and bushy tail in one or other of the rooms; they were always welcome guests, allowed to move quite freely through the house, so she was not apprehensive about snakes. She loved it all and she was particularly fond of their kitchen garden in which vegetables grew so well. They had very large marrowfat peas and particularly fine watercress, whilst carrots were so plentiful they used to feed them to their horses, which kept their coats in splendid condition. There was no lack of domestic staff in the household of a senior official where in those days it was not unusual to find up to forty servants – far more than in our time, but easy to appreciate against a background of organisation which never allowed one man to do more than one job. The list was therefore formidable: bearers, cooks, *chowkidar* (watchmen), gardeners, syces (grooms), *kidmatgar* (waiters), *misalchi* (dishwasher), *dhobi* (washermen or women), *ayah*, (nursemaids), sweepers, cowmen, *murghi-wala* (poultry-keepers) and the inevitable verandah *dharzi* (tailor). Even now I have omitted the *tum-tum wala* (groom who looked after the various horse-drawn vehicles). Evidently Fanny took little part in the day-to-day management of their house and staff, of which Robert, with his *abdar* (butler), took charge.

27

My grandfather's work at Allahabad was a new experience for him; his venue was now mainly urban and he was involved, particularly as a magistrate, in all measures for the detection and prevention of hideous crimes like infanticide and *thagi*. He was head of the Criminal Justice Department and of the police force of his city and district, where, shortly after he arrived, there was a ghastly famine; the monsoons failed, the Ganges rose only fourteen instead of the usual twenty-four feet, there was little rice or grain to be had in the markets, and armed men roamed everywhere in search of plunder. One day a Hindu Rajput was brought before him, charged with the deliberate murder of his wife and daughter. The man admitted that he had killed them both by cutting off their heads with his sword, but he knew his wife had been unfaithful to him and therefore he killed her. He supposed, inevitably, that 'the magistrate Sahib Bahadur' would now kill him for the act, and as in that case his young daughter would find no one to marry her, and would be obliged to beg for food (which, because of the famine, did not exist), he killed her also.

Unfortunately I have no record of my grandfather's comment, verdict, or sentence on this (orientally well-reasoned!) case. There are also no copies of letters which he wrote to his subordinates at this time, but the official reports about him refer to his great energy, his hard work and the long hours he spent in office. Henry Carre Tucker, his great friend who had succeeded him as Collector at Azamgarh, wrote to him about this:

2nd Feb 1839 Azamgarh

My dear Monty

I quite pity your present labours, but however disagreeable for the present I dare say they will do you a great deal of good by fairly routing you out and making you exert both mind and body to the uttermost! Poor staid old Monty, conceive him going up to Cutcherry [the office] at 4 a.m. in the morning! You're surely not in ernest when you ask me whether I would go to Allahabad, now that I am master of Azamgarh, independently, in my own right. I like to stay at the old place and make it the best zillah [district] in the country.

Ever yours affectly
Carre Tucker

Give my kindest regards to Mrs Montgomery.

This letter confirms how poor Fanny also suffered at Allahabad from Robert's prolonged absence at his daily work. He was always addressed now as 'Monty' though my father recorded that the nickname was pronounced in those days 'Munty', and that at Harrow he himself was known as 'Munty'.

In spite of his many commitments, both official and domestic, Robert remained astonishingly fit at Allahabad, which had a bad reputation for malaria, or jungle fever as it was called, as well as the typhoid from which Fanny suffered so much. Some forty years were to pass before Sir Ronald Ross traced malaria to the anopheles mosquito, and the remedies practised by doctors in India at that time seem extraordinary now. Apparently there were two recognised 'cures' for malaria: blood letting by use of a lancet or drinking large quantities of claret! Whilst the Montgomerys were at Allahabad the Head of the Government Customs Service there had a serious attack of 'fever' and the local doctor advised the claret treatment. The patient had to drink a bottle a day, whilst his head was enveloped in three 'bladders of ice' and iced towels were wrapped round his neck. The hot weather had begun, so much precious ice must have been used on this patient, but the Chief Customs Officer was always very popular! Apparently, after three weeks on a diet solely of claret and fresh straw-berries, and with the aid of two British artillerymen from Allahabad Fort who 'nursed' him with the iced towels, this officer made an excellent recovery[7]!

As Collector of a great city my grandfather appeared frequently in public and had to speak on formal occasions, including making speeches after public dinners or ceremonies. He and Fanny were of like mind in their religious convictions, so perhaps not surprisingly he recorded extracts from his 'devotions' for use on every occasion, including public functions, which poor Fanny often could not attend. For instance:

Prayer before a Public Dinner

Lord I cast myself on Thee for discretion and support, guidance and merciful help. I am a child, I *cannot speak*. Be Thou to me a mouth and wisdom.

Afterwards

Lord, to Thee be all the praise.

The italics above are mine, for I am sure he knew his speech would be a success, which it clearly was from his thanks to the Almighty! A little over a century later we saw this same religious attitude reflected in Robert Montgomery's grandson, when, on the evening before Alamein, Monty called on 'The Lord Mighty in battle'.

At this time Fanny was corresponding frequently with Honoria Lawrence at Ferozepore where the latter's husband, Sir Henry, was Agent for the Governor-General in the Punjab (Punjab was still an independent Sikh Kingdom). Honoria was the daughter of the Rector of Carndonagh, a village in Inishowen only ten miles from Moville, and so was well known to all Robert's family. She was devoted to Fanny though unlike her in many ways, for Honoria was in no way shy and contributed articles to

The Calcutta Review, one of which excited considerable attention when she wrote:

> Did the Court of Directors of our Company but understand their real interests, as well as the Athenians did theirs, they might perhaps make it imperative that their officers should, on entering the service, be provided with a wife.

One letter that Honoria wrote to Fanny is important to this story:

Ferozepore
17th Jany 1842

My dearest Friend [she always wrote thus to Fanny]

You will have seen enough in the papers perhaps to judge of our dreadful anxiety – George Lawrence taken prisoner, his fate unknown. Our darling boy has again been very ill with dysentery, and is much reduced, but I trust the complaint is stopped. However I ought to complain of no personal anxiety while Henry continues well, and he was so on the 10th, still at Peshawar, and the further movements of Colonel Wilde's Brigade undecided.

I took up the pen, however, to tell you that your brother James has got into the Commissariat (Supply) department – a good step for him and a good addition to his salary I fully believe. I saw the order tonight appointing your brother temporarily to the post of Commissariat Officer at Peshawar, and there is no doubt of it being confirmed. I long to hear from you, my dear friend. These are dreadful times for us all. Captain Trevor who was murdered at the same time as the 'Envoy' had his wife and 5 children at Kabul.

Yours most affectionately,
H. Lawrence

Best kisses and wishes to the dear babes.

'These dreadful times' to which Honoria referred were the awful disasters of the First Afghan War, when the 'Envoy', Sir William Macnaughton, with Sir Alexander Burns and seven other British officers, had been murdered in the Residency at Kabul in December 1841. What followed is history; how the garrison (5000 fighting men including 1000 Europeans with 12,000 camp followers) endeavoured to withdraw to Peshawar but was totally destroyed, and how only one survivor (an Englishman Dr Brydon) was left alive to tell the tale. George Lawrence, with twenty other British officers and all the wives and children of the garrison, had been kept as hostages by the Afghans. Eight months after Honoria wrote this letter George Lawrence was released when General Pollock invaded Afghanistan and reoccupied Kabul. George was the second of the five Lawrence brothers and an officer in the 2nd Light Cavalry. Robert wrote of him:

He had not the genius of Henry and John but he was a splendid man, and, from his pay, financed the education of his two younger brothers. He was a little, burly fellow ('Cocky' Lawrence we called him) and he did well, ending as Sir George Lawrence, KCSI, CB.

The record of these three brothers may well be unique. Sir Henry, selected as first Viceroy of India but killed before he could assume office; Lord (John) Lawrence became Viceroy; and the second eldest, became General Sir George Lawrence.

Victorian families looked on brothers-in-law as natural brothers and 'your brother James', to whom Honoria referred in her letter to Fanny, was James Montgomery, eight years younger than his brother Robert. James had been nominated (of course by Josias Dupré Alexander!) for a commission as ensign in the Company's military service and had joined the 60th Bengal Native Infantry direct from Foyle College. The first reaction by Robert to his younger brother's commission was the realisation that money due to him following the death of his parents (they had both died in Ireland some years earlier), would not now be paid. His elder brother Samuel, who was Rector of a parish in Co. Londonderry and had inherited the Moville property, had sent him the following letter:

26th December 1837

My dear Robert

Before this letter reaches India you will I hope have seen James.

I had a letter from you dated 26th July in which you desired me to pay you the money left after the death of our father and mother. But the balance in my hands amounts to some £150, and, as you desired me to do what I thought best with it, I applied it to help pay the expenses of sending James out. I was obliged to raise some £400/500 to do this but the rest shall be lodged for you in the Provincial Bank, so that it will always be increasing a little.

Believe me to be, yours very afftly
Samuel Montgomery

After receiving this letter Robert recorded, understandably perhaps, that he found it rather difficult to determine the amount of money due to him. In any case it was all withheld and he saw none of it! Lack of money certainly continued in our family during the next hundred years, for, at the risk of a personal interlude, it fell to me to experience its impact beyond doubt. As the youngest of nine children, when the time came for me to enter Sandhurst the family money available for outfitting and the like was running short. So far I had never worn new trousers, always those handed down to me by one of my five brothers, and when I reported as a new cadet at the Royal Military College I had on a pair of my brother Bernard's. Of course I did not know then that I was wearing the trousers of an officer who was to become a Field-Marshal and one of the greatest of military leaders! No such thought occurred to me, for I was preoccupied, as I gazed with envy at the obviously new outfits of other junior cadets, with the thought that someone might discover I did not have any new trousers. For that I had to wait till I was commissioned.

Great Uncle James' military career was short and tragic, like that of so many young infantry officers in the Company's armies. He was eighteen when he joined the 60th Bengal Native Infantry, and in 1839 was with the Field Force sent to capture the Rani of Jhansi and annex her State. Apparently he was not at all pleased by the lack of resistance to the expedition for he wrote home to say:

The Rani and all her followers made away during the night, and at 8 o'clock we and the 25th marched into Jhansi Fort thinking we were going to fight. I have since been all over the Fort which is a strong place, and the defenders might have shown us some good fun, if they had stood firm and fought.

There was no need for his disappointment as he soon became involved in the military disasters of that First Afghan War. On 19th January 1842, two days after Honoria Lawrence wrote to Fanny Montgomery, he was wounded during an unsuccessful attempt to secure the Khyber Pass. Apparently he was not confirmed in that Commissariat appointment and had rejoined his regiment in time to take part in very fierce fighting, in which he was shot in the thigh by an Afridi tribesman; that day his battalion had ten men killed and eighty other casualties. Evidently his wound was not serious as he was with the 60th during all the subsequent operations of General Pollock's army, until just before the capture of Kabul on 15th September. Three days before that he was wounded again, in a hard-fought battle against 5000 Afghans, to force the Tezin Pass and break out of the mountain barrier that barred the way to the capital.

Light khaki cloth (drill) uniform did not appear for another fifteen years (at the time of the Mutiny) and the Company's armies, with all British troops, still wore their red, blue or green dress tunics, with regimental facings, on every occasion - parade or exercise, in peace or war. The regiments of the Bengal Army were famous for their magnificent uniforms'. Infantry sepoys generally wore scarlet tunics, with two leather cross belts and a waist belt (fastened by a brass plate and all pipeclayed white), white trousers and a high dark blue shako embossed with the regimental number; they carried the Brown Bess musket and a long bayonet, with a cartridge box for sixty rounds of ammunition, a water bottle and a knapsack. How they climbed and fought in mountain warfare is a marvel! British officers wore scarlet tunics with a high collar and epaulettes, a tall shako or forage cap, and long white overalls, and were armed with sword and pistol.

In the India Office Library there is a pen and ink and water-colour sketch, with other drawings of the First Afghan War, entitled: 'Action in the Tezin Pass.' The sketch is beautifully executed, and portrays a scene of frontier warfare so familiar to all who served on the North-West Frontier Province. A rough road, little more than a track, is seen winding its way through a defile towards the summit of the Pass that gave access to the Kabul River Valley. A long column of troops with artillery and transport (camels, horses, pack mules and ox-carts) is travelling along the road or astride it; at one point there is a dry river bed, rock-strewn and difficult with steep banks, and men are pushing and hauling to help get the vehicles across. A section of Foot Artillery, two six-pounder guns drawn by bullocks, with the artillerymen (always Europeans) on foot, has pulled out of the column and is at 'Action Stations' in case it is urgently needed. In the right foreground, on a high ridge overlooking the road, there is a large stone-built sangar (or breastwork) occupied by an infantry picquet; they are there to protect the route from attack or ambush, by the tribesmen, who can be seen watching the column from various heights covering the Pass. Evidently this picquet has already been attacked and there has been fierce hand-to-hand fighting; for there are bodies of tribesmen nearby who have obviously been bayoneted by the scarlet-clad sepoys, some of whom lie dead inside the sangar. An officer, with his sword drawn, is inside the picquet and clearly another attack is expected; the sun is setting and it is a time of great danger.

Looking closely at this sketch I felt sure the artist knew that the 60th Bengal Native Infantry were finding the picquets for Tezin Pass on 12th September 1842; indeed I persuaded myself I could see their distinctive (Saxon green) facings on the scarlet uniforms of the officer and his sepoys, For Great Uncle James was on picquet duty in the Pass that day. His company was attacked that very night and had five men killed and seventeen wounded out of eighty; and he himself was hit and disabled by a musket ball in the left forearm. That was the end of James' military career, for he never really recovered from his two wounds and privation. He was not evacuated to India as no sick and wounded could be sent back through the passes still held by hostile tribesmen. In any case in those days the ambulance service was very primitive, and if you were not 'walking wounded' you were lucky to be conveyed in a bullock cart, or in a *doolie* carried by four bearers, or unlucky if you were on a stretcher, tied in, on the back of a camel - a fearful fate indeed! So James marched back with his regiment when the army withdrew to Peshawar, with little opposition, reaching there in November. Reaction then set in and he was sent off to Simla on sick leave, apparently in very poor shape. It is surprising he was sent there, for Simla, the first hill station to be built, can be extremely cold in winter and maybe that is why he never recovered. He died there on 18th April 1843 suffering, according to the official report, from 'wounds

33

and hardship'; he was only twenty-five. One hundred and ten years later I found his Afghan War medal, engraved on the reverse side 'Cabool 1842' but minus its ribbon and with the suspension bar broken, lying unwrapped in a chest of drawers that came to me when our Irish home was sold.

Young James was not the only member of Robert's family in India at this time. His sister Anne Alexander, a year older than himself, had arrived in Bengal while he was at Azamgarh. Anne had inherited all her mother's good looks and was tall, slight and graceful. After an unhappy affair with a near neighbour of her family in Moville, she had met and married Alexander Charles Heyland, who was much older, and on leave from Bengal where he was a member of the Company's Civil Service. He was a protégé and cousin of the influential Josias Dupré Alexander, who once again had exercised his patronage in favour of a relative!

When the Montgomery's arrived at Allahabad, Alexander Heyland was the Judge at Ghazipore on the Ganges, downstream from Benares, and Fanny used to visit her sister-in-law, travelling in one of the Allahabad Collector's boats. Navigation on both the Jumna and Ganges was always very difficult because the channels were continually changing their course, with unpredictable, very strong, and often dangerous currents. The time had not yet come when the Collector would have his own steam launch, and for his official journeys on the rivers Robert had a boat fitted with a keel and propelled by oars or sails, with a native crew of up to ten men. Otherwise it was the custom when with one's family, or on long journeys, to travel in country boats, which were large, flat-bottomed and therefore very cumbersome craft. Houses or shelters made of matting and bamboo, roofed with thatch, were erected on the decking, though in storm or high wind this actually hampered navigation. Boat journeys were therefore slow and a pukka sahib, travelling by river with his family or friends, would certainly never have less than three boats; one for the travellers, followed by the cook-boat to convey the servants, food, and the poultry in charge of the *murghi-wala* (the latter travelled on the roof of the bamboo shelter with his chickens, ducks, turkeys, etc.). A horse boat came last with the syces, *tum-tums*, and harness – in case one or more of the *sahib-log* wished to land, and ride or drive for the next stage. By land from Allahabad to Ghazipore was 90 miles, by water the distance was 150 miles.

Fanny always enjoyed her boat journeys, particularly for the peace of it and the ever-changing sights, so different from the sameness of Azamgarh District. The river scene enchanted her. There were always ferry boats carrying passengers, with cows and buffaloes swimming in tow. Sometimes elephants, with their trunks held high and carrying their mahouts (who were always talking to them), swam the ferry crossing; for the elephant is a marvellous swimmer, perhaps the best of all the mammals after the whale. Then she passed enormous boats loaded with cotton, going downriver to

Calcutta, and these often got stuck on sand banks, dislodging several great crocodiles that had been basking in the sunshine.

Most of all Fanny loved the fascination of the 'bend in the river'. What would appear next for her pleasure? It might be high tree-clad cliffs, revealing, in an open space, a cluster of beautiful Hindu temples, the whole reflected in the sun-lit river; or a village teeming with life, with children bathing and shouting. Sometimes a string of camels would appear, proceeding at a long swinging trot, occasionally each one ridden by a cameleer. Then, in the evening, peacocks began calling from the cliffs and often came down to feed by the riverside. They took no notice of men, and for this the *murghi-wala* was very glad as they made such good eating. Once only they passed the Calcutta steam boat, with her two great paddle wheels threshing the water and tall funnel belching smoke, her deck thronged with passengers. Often a corpse floated quietly down the Ganges, but Fanny was quite used to that. Then came the final bend and there was Ghazipore, with the attractive pukka houses of the Civil Lines built alongside the river bank, and Annie waving to her from the steamer 'Ghat', or landing place.

Fanny did not visit Ghazipore after 1839, for in that year death came to her sister-in-law. Annie Heyland already had three children, born at yearly intervals in 1835, '36 and '37, and two years later she died after a still-born birth. A tragic story, yet by no means unusual; it resembled that of many young people who went out to India in the heyday of the East India Company. For them, as in our time, India was fascinating, attractive and beautiful, almost fearful in its vastness; yet all-pervading in thought and action, and overlaid with glamour. When sickness, disease, sudden death, separation or loneliness intervened (worse still if poverty came your way) the glamour and attraction began to wear thin. But Annie's marriage had never been a success; in reality she and her husband shared little except the same Christian name of Alexander.

My grandfather only once saw his sister Annie at Ghazipore; he was too much taken up with his work and had no time to leave his district, except on official business. The impact of the Afghan War emphasised the need for Bengal's communications with and through the Punjab, and he became much involved in the construction, through his district, of the Grand Trunk Road to Peshawar, and the improvement of the waterways. He was particularly fascinated by the concept of the great highway that led to the North West Frontier; it so soon became a true image of the real India, presenting the sights and sounds, the colours and smells, as well as the happiness and sorrows, of so many different races in the subcontinent. Meanwhile Allahabad was becoming more and more important and by the early eighteen-forties two departments of the Government of India were established there. The Board of Revenue, brainchild of that expert administrator R. Mertins Bird, a predecessor of Thomason, had always been at Allahabad and now it was joined by the Department for the Suppression of Thagi and Dacoity under Major (later Sir Henry) Sleeman. Robert's commitments thus brought him in contact with senior officials, including Thomason again who had been appointed Lieutenant-Governor of the North-Western Provinces at Agra. As this story unfolds we shall see my grandfather increasingly involved in and between extremes of conflicting policies, and sometimes appearing in the role of mediator. The disparate views of Sleeman and Thomason, the grave disputes between two of the Lawrence brothers (Henry and John) in the Punjab, disapproval of military action, and the pros and cons of admitting Christian converts to a government service otherwise wholly Hindu or Muslim, are examples of problems that were to come his way. But above all the time was the run-up to the great sepoy mutiny in Bengal, and the participants, British and Indian, were gathering on the stage of events in which so many ordinary people, of different colour and race, were caught up and destroyed. My grandfather had a place on this stage; but before these great issues were decided major changes occurred in the pattern of his own life.

In the Ganges Valley the monsoon rains of 1841 were very heavy and, at Allahabad, were followed by a particularly unpleasant black ant invasion. It was not unusual, but Fanny always looked on this often annual incursion with disgust and apprehension. She had none of the insecticides we have now come to rely upon, and there was little she could do to stop pests of any kind; evidently she viewed much of her life in India as a constant battle against mosquitoes, flies and fever, with scorpions, devouring ants and every kind of loathsome bug as particular enemies after the monsoons. She sometimes woke in the morning to find the floor black with crawling monsters, which bit her ferociously; worse still it was hard to keep them off her bed, and only by spreading quicklime freely was there any hope of defeating them. No wonder she longed for the short but cold winter months when ants everywhere go to sleep.

However, before the rains ended that year Fanny knew she was pregnant again, and in the following March she miscarried; all might have been well, until suddenly the dreaded smallpox struck her (vaccination was not practised in India in her day) and she died on 23rd March 1842. She was buried at Allahabad, leaving Robert with three young children – a son, Robert, aged six years, and two daughters Frances and Mary, six and three years old respectively. Looking again at this short story of Fanny Montgomery, she was only twenty-six when she died, it is clear she was never able to come to terms with the life in India of her generation. The entry she made in her diary on her last birthday, 1st February, just seven weeks before she died, speaks for itself: 'May this year now entered upon be better than those that have gone.'

Many kind friends tried to help Robert in his new predicament, especially Lady (Henry) Lawrence who offered to take his three motherless children in her charge. But he made up his mind to bring them home where Fanny's sister would take care of them as they grew up. In November 1842 he and his family left Allahabad by river steamer for Calcutta, for three years' furlough in the United Kingdom. With so much sudden death all in one family, from wounds and hardship, sickness and disease, this chapter looked like ending in sorrow. But there was no need for that. Robert was resilient - a Victorian who did not mourn long, in the fashion of his time. He soon married again and had five more children - all born in India.

4
Punjab

My grandfather's three years' furlough began on 12th January 1843 when he embarked at Calcutta in the East Indiaman *Southampton*; she was a wooden ship of 1050 tons and still a sailing vessel, for as yet there were no steamships that made the long passage round the Cape. As a senior civil servant Robert found he was the 'burra sahib' on board, with the largest and best cabin to himself, and treated with deference by all other passengers; the latter included a Miss Sparrow whom he had engaged to look after his three young children until they reached England.

Poor Miss Sparrow! Apparently she earned very little for her arduous task of living and coping with a boy of six, and two girls aged seven and four, in the cramped conditions of a four month voyage by sailing ship. Robert complained of the awful monotony and of difficulty with the children, who were 'sadly off for frocks'; There were also violent storms with tremendous seas that caused trouble and alarm. However after St. Helena, matters improved, for he wrote: 'We went ashore and visited everything and bought everything, including 35 pounds of grapes for the rest of the voyage and cloth for the children's frocks.' They were all very glad when they disembarked at Folkestone on 4th May, and were made welcome, with great comfort, at the Royal Pavilion Hotel. From there Robert took his three children to Boulogne where George Hutchinson and his wife (Thomason's elder sister) were staying during their own furlough from India, and would look after the young Montgomerys.

My grandfather spent the next two and a half years travelling extensively in the United Kingdom and on the Continent. He wrote: 'I know nothing of British life and society and must inform myself.' He went to Shrewsbury to see the great Abbey and the tomb of Sir Roger de Montgomeri, the ancestor of all Montgomery families in the United

Kingdom. His comments on the Shropshire social scene were shrewd:

> Among the gentry there is a strong county feeling and precedence is more by residence than anything else; an Indian with a million of money would be no one, notwithstanding his birth or rank. I wanted to see what an English ball was like [Queen Victoria had just completed six years of her reign] and I was invited to a very select one, with only one hundred present, all but two of old and very respectable family. There I saw all the beauty and aristocracy of Shropshire and was never more pleased with anything of the kind, the ladylike appearance of the girls was most striking, their dresses most elegant without being fine or tawdry, and there was a polite ease over the whole party that I never before witnessed. There was no vulgarity, no boisterous rudeness or mirth, but a grace and loveliness that was charming.

Of course in Ireland he found matters rather different!

> I crossed to Waterford and on to Kilkenny, to Lord Desart's[9] place, where I attended the servants' ball, dancing one set (of Lancers) with the cowherd's wife and another (of the Irish hornpipe) with the dairy maid.

He returned to Liverpool from Londonderry in an Irish cattle boat with a deck cargo of 450 pigs, 100 sheep, 45 bullocks and 3000 geese; there was a terrible storm and the voyage took three days!

In London Robert called at East India House, in Leadenhall Street, and saw the magnificent way in which the Court of Directors conducted their business. He was not surprised by the importance of the doorkeepers, in their uniform of chocolate-coloured frock-coat, with red collar and waistcoat, black cloth trousers and cocked hat, who so resembled his office *chaprassi* in India; a visiting high official (a provincial Governor or a general) must pay the doorman at least £20, whilst even a Collector must pay £5, to get any proper attention!

In the last year of his furlough my grandfather met his second wife whom he married in London on 2nd May 1845. She was Miss Ellen Jane Lambert, not quite twenty-one years old on her wedding day. Fortunately she was no stranger to India, where her father had been a Calcutta merchant, as she was born at Arrah on the Ganges, only about 100 miles downstream from Ghazipore. The Lamberts were an old English family who had lived in Woodmansterne, Surrey, for centuries. Their eldest daughter, Ellen, was a beautiful girl with dark brown hair, a high intelligent forehead and full mouth, large grey eyes and wonderful colouring. She was completely different from Robert's first wife, being strong physically, very determined and not shy in any way; she was a powerful character, full of common sense, and always had great influence on my grandfather and her children. Throughout her life, after her marriage, she remained firmly opposed to any mention of Fanny Montgomery in her presence!

Robert returned to India with his new wife early in 1846 and, through the influence of Thomason, still Lieutenant-Governor at Agra, was appointed Magistrate and Collector of Cawnpore, another great city on the Ganges. There he was soon caught up in the political and military scene that was unfolding in Northern India at this time.

Ranjit Singh, the one-eyed 'lion of the Punjab,' who had defeated both the Great Mogul and the Afghans to form an independent Sikh Kingdom, had died. He was an adventurer who had won his place by the sword and kept it by force during his lifetime, but he was always friendly with the British and took care never to make war against them. After his death six years of anarchy followed in the Punjab, and then the Sikh army, a magnificent force which Ranjit Singh had spent his life in training, crossed the Sutlej and invaded the North-Western Provinces in November 1845. Lord Hardinge, a splendid old soldier and no longer young, for he had served in the Peninsular Wars and had been wounded four times, was the Governor-General. This was the start of the first Sikh War which saw hard and bitter fighting between the 60,000 Sikh warriors, with their 150 guns, and the sepoys of the Company's Bengal Army under Lord Gough, the Commander-in-Chief. Victory for the Company's army came early in February at the decisive and bloody engagement at Sobraon, where one quarter of the Sikh army perished in the Sutlej River, and old Lord Hardinge fought alongside the sepoys in the ranks. The turning point of the campaign for the British had been the arrival of a great column of elephants and 4000 ox-carts, laden with ammunition and supplies, sent by John Lawrence from Delhi where he was the Collector and Magistrate. A by-product of this war was the folly of the British when they installed a Hindu (a Dogra Rajput, the Prince Gulab Singh of Jammu) as Maharajah of all Kashmir, a Hindu ruler of a predominantly Muslim people. We sold the sovereignty of that lovely land for one million pounds, and lived to regret it! This was just at the time when Robert Montgomery went to Cawnpore, and Henry Lawrence to Lahore (as Resident) to see whether peace with the Sikhs, after their defeat, could be preserved; meanwhile John Lawrence administered the Punjab district of the Jullundur Doab between the Sutlej and Ravi rivers.

Now Thomason appears, and in a vital role. The Doab was a new commitment and both Henry and John Lawrence had to have able assistants to administer fresh territory. So Thomason sent experts from the North Western Provinces, all men trained by himself, like Lumsden (he had already raised The Guides), George Lawrence, Herbert Edwardes, Reynell Taylor, Lake, Abbott, Bowring, Richard Pollock and John Becher. Then the second Sikh War began. The Sikh nation did not consider itself defeated and in 1848 its army rose once more to avenge Sobraon, precipitating a conflict no less desperate that that of 1845–46, though shorter with very heavy casualties, particularly at Chillianwallah, and the final British victory at the battle of Gujerat early in 1849. By now Lord Dalhousie had succeeded Hardinge as Governor-General and one of his first acts was to send Sir Henry Elliot formally to annex the whole Punjab under British rule. The new province was huge, for it included virtually all of what in our day (and now) was the North West Frontier Province, with the Derajat and all Trans-Indus territory up to Peshawar and beyond. Once more the influence of Thomason is seen, and again he sends his best officers from the North-Western Provinces to assist in the settlement of the Punjab. This second instalment, the 'Punjab set' they were called, included Richard Lawrence, and men like Chamberlain, Macpherson, George Barnes, Cust, Forsyth, Brendreth, Charles Raikes, Thornton, Hodson (of Hodson's Horse) and Robert Montgomery.

In all Thomason released twenty-eight officers for the Punjab. More than half came from either the nine counties of Ulster or from Scotland, and all were very strong Protestants, akin to Thomason in their religious convictions; they were either civil servants trained at Haileybury or soldiers of the Bengal Army seconded for civil duties, but, to quote from Sir Charles Oman's *History of England*: 'The officers to whom the settlement of the Punjab was given over were the picked men of India.' This was very fortunate because, in the aftermath of the two Sikh Wars, the settlement problems were complicated by the facts of a diverse population – militant Sikhs, smarting from their defeat, mingled with Muslims and Hindus. After the Sikh Wars, and very sensibly as it turned out, some complete Sikh regiments (notably the Ferozepore and Ludhiana Sikhs) were raised as infantry for the Bengal Army, and Sikhs were recruited for the Punjab Police and government service.

My grandfather had spent only two years at Cawnpore before his promotion and transfer to the Punjab as Commissioner of the Lahore Division. He was now a very senior official and was able to build his own house in the Civil Lines at Anarkulli, large enough for himself and Ellen and his growing family of children.

My grandfather left a plan of this house which showed it as a rectangular-shaped bungalow, in the then new fashion for senior officers, brick-built with four tall chimneys and a tiled and gabled roof, the pitch of which was well designed to stand the stress of monsoon storms; a handsome flat-roofed and colonnaded portico led through a wide verandah and the front doorway into an entrance hall 18ft square, beyond which were the main drawing room and dining room, each 30ft by 20ft. The interior kept very much to one pattern, with large rooms, high ceilings and plain whitewashed walls, which made for coolness and accentuated the impression of spaciousness. A wide verandah, supported by Mughal-style arches, ran all round the outside of the house with entrance doors leading to every room, all of which were built adjoining the central feature of the main living rooms; there were six bedrooms each with its own bathroom, though of course there was then no piped water supply and a 'bathroom', though measuring 20ft by 18ft, meant only a hip-bath and a 'thunder-box'! The kitchens were quite separate buildings at the rear, near the servants' quarters.

This house, named 'New Park' after Robert's family home, stood well back from the road within its own walled compound, enclosing the large garden with its deep well and Persian water wheel, and of course the stables. In its general style this type of residential bungalow changed very little during the whole time of the Raj, as readers with general knowledge of Northern India will no doubt recognise. In later years, when so much rebuilding was done, New Park, in Anarkulli, became the Lahore residence of the Nawab of Bahawalpur. Bishop Montgomery, who was born in Cawnpore in 1847 and sent back to school in England before the Mutiny, returned to Lahore for the first time fifty-eight years later, in 1913, and had no difficulty in finding 'New Park' again in the old Civil Lines. On a side of the main wall was an inscription; 'The residence of Sir Robert Montgomery 1849'.

Even after such a lapse of time the house was just the same, not changed in any way, and the bishop went straight to his old bedroom with the nursery next door; there in a corner was the thermantidote, apparently still in working order after over half a century. Robert and Fanny had a thermantidote at Allahabad, but there is no mention of one at Azamgarh. The thermantidote was an ingenious apparatus, hand operated as the punkah was, in order to cool the air when the house temperature could be well over 90°F. In our time we hung long cuscus tatties (or matting of cuscus-grass) over the doorway and kept them constantly wet to reduce the temperature. The thermantidote comprised a wood frame on which a light metal fan was mounted close to the tatties, and geared to a wheel; as long as this wheel was kept turning the fan rotated, and drew a constant stream of cool air into the house. It sounds effective enough and presumably was so, but the motive (engine) power was a coolie and it must have been far more arduous than the *punkah-wala*'s task!

After 1848 Ellen Montgomery always went for the hot weather to the new hill station at Dharmsala, where Robert joined her as often as he could. Her two teenage step-daughters went with her as well as her four young sons - Arthur, Henry, James and Ferguson. All her sons were born in the six years between 1846 and 1852, but that was no trouble to Ellen; her last child (a daughter named Lucy) was born in 1856, twelve months to a day before the Mutiny began.

Before the coming of railways and motor transport, 'going to the hills' for the hot weather invariably posed big problems of organisation and method, tact and tolerance, all generally left to the memsahib to solve. To move a family like Ellen's, consisting of Robert and herself, two teenage girls, four young boys, several ayahs and all those forty or more servants, together with the household furniture (including blankets, beds and a piano), plus linen, silver, glass, cutlery, and clothing, probably required up to fourteen camels apart from pack ponies, mules and ox-carts. In those very early days fully-furnished accommodation, hotels and guest houses, etc., did not exist in the hills. The family themselves generally travelled in buggies and their food for the journey, generally about thirteen miles a day, had to be arranged, including nights spent in camp, either in tents or at a dak bungalow. Their retinue of servants marched on foot with the camels and slow transport, and trouble began when a cook, or some key servant, fell out or otherwise could not complete a march. And of course the whole process, and journey, had to be repeated some five months later when all the *sahib-log* returned to the plains in September.

The final stage of these annual journeys to Dharmsala began at Pathankot (the railhead in our time), where so many families met and rested before starting on their last lap to the foothills and the mountain resort. However, the difficulties and frustrations of these family moves, twice a year, were always well worthwhile including the prospect, or memory, of the very gay social life at a hill station. The climate was perfect after the humidity of the plains, the scenery was superb, and there was plenty of scope, and time, for amateur theatricals, picnics, dances, concerts, riding in the hills and (even more important) the company of the wives, daughters and female friends of British officers.

While he was Commissioner of the Lahore Division my grandfather had his first meeting with the Governor-General Lord Dalhousie, an experience which brought him substantial dividends. In the winter of 1850 Dalhousie made a point of touring the Punjab, his recently annexed province, and spent much time at Lahore; after which he invited Gulab Singh, the Maharajah of Kashmir, to pay him a state visit at Wazirabad. This town is on the Indian side of the frontier, and of the road that threads its way through the high mountains of Jammu and the Banihal Pass into the Vale of Kashmir. For this meeting with the Maharajah, Lord Dalhousie took with him both the Lawrence brothers (Sir Henry and John), Sir Henry Elliot, and Robert Montgomery, together with an imposing escort that included the 9th Lancers, three British infantry battalions, horse artillery, Bengal cavalry, and the Governor-General's Band. Much ceremony and protocol was observed, and Dalhousie and his staff, including Robert, rode to their first meeting with the Maharajah in full dress uniform, all mounted on elephants (twenty-one in number). Gulab Singh was attended by only 2500 troops of his own army, as two of his infantry regiments had been delayed by terrible snow storms in the Banihal where they lost fifty men. That Banihal Pass! Some readers will recall the great difficulties they experienced even in our day with motor transport, when returning by road from Srinagar over the Banihal, 9000 feet above sea level, to Lahore.

Of course magnificent gifts were presented to, and accepted by, each side at the Grand Durbar at Wazirabad; for that occasion Gulab Singh arrived mounted on his state elephant, and seated in a howdah made of solid silver. Robert's share of the Maharajah's gifts included a Kashmir shawl of the finest quality, valued even in those far off days at £100. Whether he should have kept it is another matter! However Bishop Montgomery found it in 1920, quite untouched and still in its original wrapping. He and my mother then 'sold it to an American friend' - but for how much there is no record!

It was after this visit to Kashmir that Lord Dalhousie wrote a report about Robert to the Court of Directors at East India House in London, couched in terms of almost embarrassing praise, such as: 'Mr Montgomery's able and admirable exertions have produced a success which may well seem marvellous'. My grandfather had a complete copy of this report, but one wonders how he got it!

During this time at Lahore Robert began to appreciate the awful plight of the soldiers, and their wives and children, in the British regiments, who had to stay in the plains during the hot weather. Their officers could go to the hills, but not they, and the mortality rate among the females was reckoned, on average, at fifty British wives and one hundred children annually, chiefly due to cholera, malaria and typhoid. The only way to remedy this appalling state of affairs was to send the sick to the hills, but so far Government had found it too expensive to accept the commitment. Robert noted in his papers: 'In proof of the scarcity of English women, and the mortality among soldiers, you may see a soldier's wife with wedding rings reaching up to the joint of her finger'! It took him nearly ten years to get matters changed, and it was not until 1862, when he was Lieutenant-Governor of the Province, that he was able to establish a permanent summer camp for soldiers' families at Muree, 5300 feet above sea level.

By now the wheel of fortune had turned full circle from the days of Foyle College and four of the Lawrence brothers, with my grandfather, were serving in the Punjab. Furthermore, Robert had been promoted again and had joined Henry and John Lawrence as a member of the three-man Board of Administration, set up by Lord Dalhousie to govern the province, with Sir Henry as its President. Henry, a soldier of the Bengal Artillery and the senior of the three men, was responsible for all military, political and diplomatic business. He had always opposed annexation, holding strongly that the Punjab should remain a buffer state against the turbulent Pathans of the North West Frontier, and the Sikhs in particular were devoted to him; whilst Resident at Lahore he had been virtually ruler of the province. John Lawrence, Haileybury-trained and always pro-annexation, had charge of finance and land revenue tax, for which Dalhousie needed his skill and experience to produce a rapid Punjab settlement. Robert

Not always

44

Montgomery, the third member, was responsible for law and order, the police, magistracy, roads, communications and education. But Dalhousie also needed a peaceful settlement and for this he relied on Henry's influence with, and regard for, the militant Sikh element. In this difficult climate, of two ill-assorted brothers, Robert joined the Board well knowing he had great liking and affection for Henry, though in policy he was on the side of John.

Not surprisingly a governing body of this divisive nature quickly ran into trouble and very serious difficulties arose.[10] Looking back it appears all too easy to blame Dalhousie for this whole sorry affair; but so far few British writers have held either Henry or John Lawrence responsible for allowing their professional and personal differences to cloud their judgement for so long, and, above all, for being seen to do so.

With this in mind I read my grandfather's description of the grave friction that developed between the Lawrence brothers at Lahore. Each complained about the other in long letters to Robert, and eventually the two brothers refused to meet, and communicated only through Robert. Unfortunately their letters of this time (the original manuscripts) were in the volume of my grandfather's papers most eaten by mice. Those from John Lawrence, and he wrote far fewer letters than his brother, have been virtually obliterated, but obviously he was attacking Henry to my grandfather. Henry Lawrence wrote at great length, sometimes a letter of six foolscap pages, and he always gave only the date of the month, never the year. An extract from one such letter (of Henry's) will suffice to show the near absurdity of the position, particularly as Henry was President of the Board, and therefore John's boss, and that he asked Robert to show the letter to John. This letter must have been written during the hot weather of 1852, when the shade temperature was probably 100° Fahrenheit!

Lahore
May 29

My dear Monty

I have delayed even noticing John's letter to you until I can do so quite coolly.

Assuredly John's picture of my not only having done very little myself, but of being in his way while he was doing all the work of the Board, is so far fetched that he must have been influenced by angry and jaundiced feelings. His picture would make me a clever and diseased malingerer utterly unadapted for his business ...

I observe he details several instances in which he allows he was very angry indeed. I remember some of them and can surely say I was much less angry than vexed, and that never did I intentionally behave in an offensive way, as John would imply; nor did I say or do anything that I would not have said or done to yourself under like circumstances. The chances are therefore that I

was cooler than he was and that my conduct was less offensive than his was
. . . One word more. I have now been upwards of 29 years in India, but to this
day, I have made no enemy and have had no serious quarrel. Am I, think you,
now more quarrelsome than I was at Gorakhpore or Allahabad? Why then
should I quarrel with John when I do not so with you? . . . You can show
John this, and I hope it will satisfy him that, whatever he may think of my
acts, my intentions are not evil.

Yours v. sincerely
HL

(Henry Lawrence always initialled his letters.)

    The above letter shows the depth of puerility, amounting to farce, to
which each brother descended in his detestation of the other. Their
unseemly quarrel continued for four years until 1853, when Henry
Lawrence was posted away to fill a vacancy as Governor-General's Agent
in Rajputana. Both the brothers wrote to Lord Dalhousie asking for the
appointment because, each said: 'I cannot work with my brother.' But
Dalhousie chose Henry for Rajputana and then appointed John Lawrence
to be the first Chief Commissioner for the new province of the Punjab,
with my grandfather as his Judicial Commissioner and second-in-
command.

    Before this my grandfather's sense of humour had evidently come to his
rescue when he found he was the buffer between the two Lawrence
brothers, for he wrote: 'I was like a tame elephant between two wild
buffaloes'! In fact he rather enjoyed the situation, for he added: 'The
Lawrences used to say I was the only contented man in the Punjab.'
Unfortunately Robert kept no record of the replies he wrote to their letters
to himself, but he did set down his own view of each brother at Lahore.

Montgomery's view of Henry and John Lawrence

There is no doubt that John is a tremendous worker and strong as a horse. He
can stand many more hours of actual effort than Henry, or than anyone else
out here, and he is rough. He hasn't the grace and charm of Henry. One
remembers the answer John sent to Dalhousie's secretary when the latter
asked him what sort of men he wanted for the Punjab: 'Send me men with
guts.' He probably thought Henry was lacking! Maybe he is but Henry has
beauty of mind, sympathy, imagination, courtesy, respect for all races. John is
respected: Henry is loved: Henry is generous with his money: John the
reverse.

My grandfather kept two contemporary photographs (1856) of John and
Henry Lawrence; both half-length and taken full face. John is shown with
his broad brow and lined face, strongly-marked features, and a rather
ragged moustache. His eyes are piercing and he appears to be scowling at

the camera; he wears a broad leather belt with a big brass buckle and carries a riding switch. A strong man and an implacable opponent one would think. Henry is shown wearing an elegant coat of dark cloth with a light grey waistcoat, and neat collar and tie. He has a well trimmed beard and moustache and is wearing a cloth cap; he also has piercing eyes, but his face is long and angular and he appears deep in thought; on his coat is pinned the star of a military KCB. A kindly man one would say, but of stern purpose.

Clearly my grandfather loved his nine years at Lahore before the Mutiny, though he also suffered great loss there as the three children of his first marriage were evidently dogged by ill fortune, as their mother had been. The boy (Robert Thomason Montgomery) died aged sixteen of pneumonia, when he was at school in England preparing for Addiscombe. The eldest girl, Frances Mary, married Sir Donald McLeod when she was nineteen and he was forty-four; British girls were scarce in the Punjab and twenty-five years difference in age did not matter – at any rate not to him and we can only hope not to her! But she died within a year of her marriage. McLeod went to Haileybury and joined the Bengal Civil Service; like Thomason he was deeply religious, in fact even more so – what we would call a religious maniac. He had great influence with the Sikhs, and was literally worshipped by one of their sects, as an incarnation. When he finally left India a Sikh chieftain said: 'Send us back Donald McLeod and we shall become Christians.' Nevertheless my grandfather had trouble with him later, as we shall see. Robert's younger daughter, Mary Susan, married Captain Crofton of the Bengal Engineers, when, like her sister, she was only nineteen; but she died two years later. So my grandfather very early lost all his first family, and I believe his second wife was not ill-pleased!

When Robert Montgomery became Judicial Commissioner of the Punjab it meant his days of practical work as a Collector or Deputy Commissioner were officially gone for ever; never again would he have to tour a district in order to collect revenue, act as magistrate, hunt down criminals, supervise gaols, issue excise stamps, assess for taxes, plan bridges, ferries and forests. Whenever he travelled now it would be in some state, for he was next to the Chief Commissioner, or a provincial Governor; clearly he regretted this in some ways for he wrote: 'I shall never again be able to tour my district; I shall miss the peace of a Collector's camp, remote yet never alone.' But Ellen, his second wife, was different; she liked social life as the wife of a burra sahib – besides her husband's pay was 3000 rupees a month! Also the other senior officers of government in the province were mostly old friends of the Montgomery's. The Revenue Commissioner was Donald McLeod, Robert's son-in-law. Surgeon Hathaway was Inspector of Prisons, Charles Raikes Commissioner of Lahore, Herbert Edwardes Commissioner at Peshawar and Richard Lawrence the Chief of Police. Robert Napier (later Field-Marshal Lord Napier of Magdala) was the Provincial Chief Engineer, assisted by Alec Taylor.

One of Robert's chief commitments as Judicial Commissioner was the enactment of a legal code, with the necessary penalties, for the suppression of female infanticide. This was particularly difficult, urgent and very important for new territory, where previously this crime had been virtually custom, in tune with a native philosophy which tended to degradation of the female sex; another main task was the detection and arrest of the thugs who were still so active in the province. In these circumstances, notwithstanding his new and exalted position in the provincial hierarchy, it seems Robert could not drag himself away from all practical work, for he wrote: 'It is a strange experience driving at night in a buggy with a thug (who has turned Queen's evidence) to find out where their victims have been buried.' Scarcely a job for the Judicial Commissioner!

At this time both Dalhousie and John Lawrence were writing frequently and confidentially to my grandfather on many subjects, particularly about the selection of senior officials for important appointments; clearly Robert's role and performance as mediator in the Henry and John Lawrence row had greatly enhanced his personal prestige and reputation. Robert carefully preserved the many manuscript letters, that will only interest historians now, though their contents (all unfortunately in the half-eaten volume) would have caused acute embarrassment if released to some of his contemporaries. John Lawrence generally ended his letters to my grandfather with a postscript: 'Pray keep to yourself all I write to you.' or 'I will do nothing until I get to Lahore and can see you.'

Lord Dalhousie's anger with Henry Lawrence during the latter's presidency of the Punjab Board is very clear, though perhaps irrational, for Dalhousie had created the Board! Then suddenly, in 1853, the Commissioner of the Peshawar Division, Colonel Mackeson, was murdered as he sat in the Court of Justice by a petitioner who, whilst presenting his application pretended to faint, staggered forward and stabbed the officer in the heart with a long dagger. Unfortunately Captain James, the acting Commissioner, summarily condemned the assassin to death without any investigation or trial, and immediately there were signs of grave trouble brewing. Troops were rushed to Peshawar from Rawalpindi and it was said in the bazaars 'the frontier is ablaze'. The Judicial Commissioner was at once involved and Robert acted to restore justice. The case was retried with full and proper committal procedure, legal aid for the accused, and judge and jury. However, the assassin was still convicted of murder and hanged, after which his body was burnt and his ashes scattered - 'to prevent his place of death becoming a martyr's tomb and a place of pilgrimage, with incitement to rebellion'. Severe justice maybe, but it had the merit of success, for the frontier remained quiet and Lord Dalhousie wrote to Robert in the following terms:

Govt. House
October 8th 1853

My dear Montgomery

I am much obliged for your letter of 29th ult. I am glad to see that there is at least one man at Peshawar whose heart has not sunk into his breeches.

I am deeply disgusted with the conduct of many, including that of Captain James.

Yrs., in haste, sincerely
Dalhousie

P.S. I take all responsibility

This affair at Peshawar meant that Robert had to go there from Lahore and remain on the frontier for some time. Ellen went with him and they took their son Henry (my father, Bishop Montgomery) then a boy five years old. It was the latter's first historic recollection which he never forgot, for it involved crossing the Indus in a very unorthodox fashion, and a meeting with Sir Herbert Edwardes, newly appointed Commissioner of Peshawar. In those days there was no great rail and road bridge at Attock over the mighty Indus, just down-stream from where it is joined by the Kabul river on its southward way to the Arabian Sea; there was not even a bridge of boats then, so the river crossing was always hazardous with deep water and strong currents, increased by the river junction nearby. My father was ferried across sitting on a *charpoi* (native string bedspread) supported by floats made from inflated pig skins; two men swam alongside and brought the improvised raft over. On the west bank Edwardes greeted the party; an impressive looking man with a great black beard, sprouting and uncombed. Edwardes personified the North-Western Provinces under the British Raj; there must be comparatively few British officers who served with the army in India and did not at some time travel the metre-gauge railway (how dreadfully hot it was!) from the Indus at Kalabagh to Bannu, where 'Fort Edwardes' marked the way to Waziristan.

Meanwhile at Agra, Thomason had been writing regularly to my grandfather on both personal and professional matters, following the latter's return to India from his home furlough. It has been said that Thomason had great influence on Lord Dalhousie who, but for the former, might not have dethroned the King of Oudh in 1856 and annexed his territory. Of course Thomason had his critics, exemplified by Colonel Sleeman, who very strongly opposed any further annexation of the land. These critics were in favour of maintaining the King's rule in Oudh, believing that all necessary political and land (ownership) reform was possible without annexation, which they regarded as nothing less than illegal and unjust dispossession of property. Some even went so far as to declare that Thomason's policy might cause difficulty in the Bengal Army, in which so many Rajputs, from land-owning families, were serving. On the other hand Thomason, influenced always by his strong religious sentiments and high Christian principles, saw annexation as the way to bring peace and justice to the oppressed agrarian population of Oudh; he, and his like, held strongly that only by properly planned settlement could the village communities in Oudh be rid of the corruption enforced under the old Mughal (Muslim) rulers.

This great controversy continued during the decade before the mutiny and was finally decided in favour of Thomason, not Sleeman. The two men were so different in their characters and ideals, yet both had similar, tragic endings. Thomason died at Agra, in 1853, without knowing that he had been selected, in London, to be Governor of the Madras Presidency; he was only forty-nine. Sleeman was sick and had to leave Lucknow, where he was Resident, just before annexation of Oudh was announced. He died at sea, just four days after the announcement that the Queen had knighted him.

Against the background of the Oudh controversy I have quoted below from one of Thomason's letters to my grandfather, written shortly after the latter had been transferred to the Punjab; it shows Thomason advocating his settlement policy for new territory and is particularly relevant to Robert Montgomery, who was later to become the Chief Commissioner of Oudh.

Agra
9th April 1849

My dear Monty

You have got a stirring field in your new appointment and I wish you all success in its management. There must of course be much confusion in new conditions and you cannot expect orders to be issued with fullness and precision. I would not advise you to ask for orders. I would say – act for yourself and ask for confidence. Get your agents given to you and then place them down and work away.

I am very anxious that Lord Dalhousie should report well [to London] on the civil government of the Punjab, after all the nonsense which Sir Charles Napier has talked of its necessary failure, and the superiority of a military government. I think your own progress is quite as rapid as you could expect. Starting right from the first you have an immense advantage in your own self confidence. I should say also be content with a three or five years settlement, and don't fly at once to periods of 20 or 30 years before you know the country thoroughly. Finally here is some advice on practical matters. In opening up old canals beware of following the old lines. It is cheap at the time but you will rue it afterwards. The natives generally have no idea of selecting the best lines, which should be the highest [altitude] possible. I am glad you insist on employing local people [Muslims] of the country. I am afraid of the Hindus getting in.

> Ever yours affectionately
> James Thomason

It is interesting to see Thomason advising reticence and caution in settlement decisions; he recommends short-term tenure initially, which is far removed from the policy of arbitrary confiscation of property which has been attributed to him. Evidence of hostility between the civil administration and the military Commander-in-Chief, Sir Charles Napier, is provided, and there is a reference to Robert's immense self-confidence, which, a century later, reappeared in such marked form in Field-Marshal Montgomery's character.

Because of Thomason's great influence on his trainees, of whom my grandfather was one, this story will lack balance if it does not include actual evidence cited by his critics. The eminent historian Philip Mason has severely criticised Thomason in Volume I of his great work *The Men who Ruled India*, and also, more recently, in his *A Matter of Honour*; in this latter book Mr Mason went so far as to say of Thomason's followers ('levellers' they were called because of the imputation that they sought to abolish the nobility and the great landowning *taluqdars*, leaving nothing between the princes and peasant cultivators):

> There can be no doubt that the levellers were disinterested men of high ideas, concerned – if in a somewhat abstract way – for the good of the peasant. It can be argued that they were far-sighted statesmen, anticipating as they did the kind of reform the Indian National Congress was to take up a hundred years later. But there is a coldness about their approach and a lack of humanity; they did not understand that men like old ways best. There can surely be no doubt that their reforms helped to bring about the unease, the suspicion, and the unhappiness which are the background to the Mutiny.

The last sentence of this quotation is a very grave indictment, if only because it infers that so many distinguished officers of the Company's civil and military services (most of them named earlier in this chapter, and all Thomason trainees) were collectively and personally responsible, in large measure, for a state of affairs that caused the Indian Mutiny; not Thomason, because he died in 1853, but the officers he trained. Yet these same 'levellers' successfully pacified and settled the Punjab, applying the lessons and experience they had learnt in the North Western Provinces. Admittedly Mr Mason's argument is supported by the great nineteenth-century historian Sir William Kaye in his books on The Sepoy War.

Nevertheless there is conflicting evidence about what actually happened in Oudh in 1856. Dr Pragdish Raj, in commenting on the assertion that 'the chieftains were stripped of nearly all their villages, and a settlement made in which they were entirely left out of consideration', wrote:[11]

> 'The absence of serious opposition by the taluqdars would suggest that this picture is overdrawn. The official view of the working of Dalhousie's system can be easily contradicted by a more careful study of the evidence. Out of 23,522 villages, 13,640 were settled *with* the taluqdars, and only 9,903 with persons other than taluqdars; the taluqdars *retained* more than half the province in their possesion.'

(The italics in the above passage are mine.) Finally Bosworth Smith, in his *Life of Lord Lawrence*, wrote that Sleeman actually *recommended* annexation of Oudh.

In this story 1856 has come and gone, and 1857 (Michael Edwardes has called it the *Red Year*) is beginning. We shall see the part played in the mutiny by Robert Montgomery and how he coped with the annexation problem in Oudh.

5
Mutiny

On 30th July 1857 the disarmed 26th Bengal Native Infantry broke out from Mian Mir cantonment at Lahore. Equipped only with tulwars (sabres) and hatchets they had the advantage of numbers, and, having killed and grossly mutilated their commanding officer Major Spencer, the regimental sergeant major and two havildars, who tried to intervene, they fled northward towards Kashmir, along the left bank of the Ravi, hotly pursued on horseback by Mr Montgomery and his armed police. An unexpected dust storm (it was the monsoon season) hid the mutineers, and they were not found till next morning when they were discovered by the Tehsildar of Ajnala, who immediately attacked with his Sikh police levy and killed 150 of them; possessing no firearms, and famished, the remainder managed to swim to an island in the river. There they sheltered beneath dwarf trees and elephant grass till Mr Cooper, Deputy Commissioner of Amritzar, arrived with a strongly armed detachment of mounted (Sikh) police. Boats were procured and three hundred mutinous sepoys were brought to Ajnala, with their hands tightly pinioned, to parade in front of Mr Cooper who decided they were all murderers and must die by hanging. But there was not enough rope to hang so many, also suitable trees in the vicinity were scarce, so it was decided to shoot them all, in batches, and this was done and the bodies buried in a common pit by the village sweepers.

Later, another forty-five of the mutineers, who had escaped from the island, were captured and sent to Lahore, where they were executed by being blown from the cannon's mouth at a parade of the whole Lahore garrison, including the other disarmed native regiments, and in the presence of Mr Montgomery and senior civil officers. Thus within forty-eight hours from their quadruple murder there fell by the law nearly 500 men.

The above account might read strangely at home. But the Governors of the Punjab were of the true English stamp and mould, and knew that England expected every man to do his duty; the crime was mutiny, and even had there been no murders the punishment was death. Afterwards Mr Cooper received the following letters:

Demi-official from Sir John Lawrence, Chief Commissioner

Lahore.

2nd August 1857

Mr dear Mr Cooper

I congratulate you on your success against the 26th N.I. You and your police acted with much energy and spirit, and deserve well of the State. I trust the fate of these sepoys will operate as a warning to others . . .

Yours sincerely
John Lawrence

Demi-official from Robert Montgomery, Esq.,
Judicial Commissioner

Lahore.
Sunday 9 a.m.

Mr dear Cooper

All honour to you for what you have done, and right well you did it. There was no hesitation or delay, or drawing back. It will be a feather in your cap as long as you live . . . Better write an official report, and place the whole on record. Bring forward all who did well, and discriminate between the medium, the good, and the super excellent. You will have abundant money to reward all, and the (executioners) Sikhs should have a good round sum given to them.

There will be some stragglers; have them all picked up and send them to us. You have had slaughter enough and we want a few for the troops here, and also for evidence. The other three regiments at Mian Mir were very shaky yesterday, but I hardly think they will now go. I wish they would, as they are a nuisance, and not a man would excape if they do.

Believe me yours sincerely
R. Montgomery

(Robert's letter was written before the execution parade at Lahore.)

All the above account is taken from a long report, printed and published by the Lahore Press in 1858, entitled *Crisis in the Punjab*. The author, described only as 'A Punjab Employee' is obviously a native of the Province (probably a muslim convert to Christianity) and certainly pro-British. I have quoted it because it is entirely true, and also because it shows my grandfather's character and actions in a new light, not long after the Mutiny began in May 1857. In Chapter 3 we saw him described, by a close friend and fellow Deputy Commissioner, as 'staid old Monty', clearly at that time a very able and hardworking officer of the civil service and a strong churchman. Now he appears in an altogether different role; galloping off at a moment's notice in pursuit of mutineers-cum-murderers, and, when they have been caught, thoroughly approving of their wholesale massacre by shooting, without any trial preliminaries, followed by the execution, by being blown from guns, of another batch of sepoy mutineers from the same regiment. Chapter VI of the report was headed 'Mutiny of the 26th N.I., and Total Destruction of the Regiment'. What caused this, on the face of it very radical, change of outlook in Robert, particularly his attitude as Judicial Commissioner to summary conviction and sentence to death without trial? Of course he was not alone at that time in India in supporting and carrying out such actions, which most people today would almost certainly describe as dreadful atrocities.

Every British history book includes some account of the Indian Mutiny of 1857, and how the bold and swift measures taken in the Punjab were a key factor in British action. Robert Montgomery was primarily responsible for this action, the story of which has been frequently told by British writers[12]; but the version of it given by Indian historians of the twentieth century is probably not generally known, and I quote from one of them now. The extract below is taken from *The War of Independence* (*National Rising of 1857*) by a Hindu writer, V. D. Savarkar.

The Chief Commissioner in the Punjab, Sir John Lawrence, was sure there would be no trouble there; like other English officers he had no idea about the impending danger till the beginning of May, and he left Lahore for the summer to find the cool air of the Murree Hills.

At this time, the greater part of the Punjab army was at Mian Mir, and the Lahore fort was garrisoned by sepoys only. At Mian Mir, though the sepoys and sowars outnumbered the English soldiers, by four to one, the English officers had no suspicion about them. The Chief Officer at Lahore was one Robert Montgomery. This Montgomery and Sir John Lawrence were both trained in the school of Dalhousie, and they were gifted with coolness and courage . . . It was necessary to find out how far the spirit of national freedom existed among the sepoys of the Punjab garrison, so a Brahman detective (employed by Mr Lawrence, Captain of Police) was sent to ascertain their state of mind. This Brahman did his foul work of treachery exceedingly well and reported to Montgomery. 'Sahib, they are steeped in revolt', and so saying he put his hand to his neck. This removed the veil from the eyes of Montgomery and he saw clearly that the revolt was organised not only in Northern India, but also in the Punjab where a fire was smouldering ready to burst into flames.

Montgomery immediately ordered all the native regiments to be disarmed on 13th May in the morning at a general parade at Mian Mir. To keep the sepoys confident in their sense of security a grand ball was given to English residents. Before the Revolutionaries guessed the secret of this apparent hunting after pleasure they were suddenly surrounded by English cavalry and artillery. It was impossible for the sepoys to see through this deceit, and, when the usual parade was taking place the artillery were ordered to be in readiness to fire, and the confused Indian regiments were peremptorily ordered to give up their arms. Thousands of sepoys, indignant with rage, but over-awed by the strong force of artillery, threw down their arms and, without a word, marched away to their new lives.

This account of the disarming at Lahore was written some seventy years ago by an Indian national who clearly regarded the Great Mutiny as the first step towards Indian independence and freedom from British domination. It shows us the apparent hatred for the English that had developed in the ranks of both Hindu and Muslim sepoys and sowars, (but chiefly among the Hindus) in many regiments of the Bengal Army. It is now a matter of history and common knowledge that terrible atrocities then began and increased, *and were perpetrated by both sides alike*. We have seen how Robert Montgomery became positively involved in atrocity, yet how does his action measure against the massacre by the Nana Sahib at Cawnpore? There British children were brained by dashing them against stone walls, and two hundred English women were hacked to death, and their bodies thrown down a well; terrible atrocities occurred too on the 12th May at Delhi, where almost the entire European and Anglo-Indian population, including the missionaries, were murdered. For their part, the British were not slow to retaliate and frequently by that most barbarous method of execution - being blown away from guns. The victims were paraded to hear their crimes, conviction and sentence to death, proclaimed to their comrades-in-arms, and to their families who were forcibly brought to witness their fate. The guns (six-pounders of the European Foot Artillery) were loaded with canister-shot rammed hard down, and the gun powder charges primed, whilst the British artillerymen stood with their portfires lighted; then each victim was tied over a gun muzzle, facing outward over the parade, and the British officer in command gave the order 'Proceed'. There was a roll of drums, on the last sound of which the gun numbers thrust their portfires into the touch holes; the bodies were blown to fragments.

This macabre way of extinguishing life was not new to India, in fact the British copied it from the Mughals. But, looking back, it seems strange how often during the Mutiny high-minded and devout Christians, like John Lawrence and my grandfather, appear to have rejoiced in execution, even though it precluded all possibility of funeral rites, for Hindu and Muslim alike. On 11th June Sir John was writing to Robert from Rawalpindi, mainly about the ineptitude of military commanders, but he ended on an apparently callous note:

Nr. Pindee

11th June 1857

My dear Monty

General Johnstone has made a mess of the Mutineers at Jullundur, but not of the right kind. In spite of my orders he failed to disarm them, and then gave them his treasure chest, and though they in return gave many warnings of what would come, he took no heed. Two Native Infantry Corps and half a Corps of Regular Cavalry have escaped from Jullundur.

Marsden is a good fellow, but soft. Pearce is bumptious, he must come back. He has more wind in his head than would carry on a Dutch lugger.

I have told McLeod to go on raising as many police horse as he may consider necessary *after* consulting you. We must keep strong.

We all feel very anxious about Delhi. There is not a man of ability, or even of action, that I know of among the leading officers with the Troops. We must trust in God, but the way we manage our military affairs is distracting.

2 Subadars, 6 Havildars, 11 Naiks and 22 Sepoys were blown from guns yesterday at Peshawar.

Yours afftly.
John Lawrence

Robert Montgomery, Esq.

P.S. My letters will come addressed to me. But when you like, you may open them. If they contain secrets, you must keep the secrets!

JL

In this letter the final reference to executions looks so like a casual addition! During the Mutiny, until Delhi was recaptured in September, Lawrence scarcely ever returned to Lahore. He took overall command of the military operations from Rawalpindi, and left the business of governing the Punjab to Robert, in whom, from his postscript, he clearly had implicit trust.

Before we continue with Robert's life in the Punjab and in Oudh during the Mutiny, and how his family fared, it is worth looking again at the causes of all this tragedy. Were there reasons for it, on either side, not yet generally known or clearly seen, and what do Indian nationals now think about it, including their reasons for the rebellion's collapse?

The often told story of the issue of the greased cartridges, so repugnant to religious susceptibilities of both Hindu and Muslim soldiers, was not the real cause of the Mutiny; though the affair was generally so bungled it became the spark that set off the rebellion at Meerut on Sunday 10th May (actually the cartridges were only a mixture of vegetable oils and candle wax). Robert Montgomery's view was that for those officers who looked ahead (all too few) the cartridge business was inadvertently a godsend for it provoked a premature explosion *before* the Mutiny was ripe. This view

57

appears justified because some regiments never mutinied at all, and many thousands of Hindu and Muslim sepoys fought with incredible courage and loyalty for the British raj, and never wavered; some regiments did not rebel until September or October of that fateful year. The Indian historian, Dr Surendra Nath Sen, in his book *Eighteen Fifty-seven*[13], says that the Mutiny was definitely not a national uprising with a premeditated plan of resistance to government. The Madras Presidency was not affected at all and there were only a few sporadic outbreaks in the Bombay Army, and fortunately not among Maratha regiments. The mutineers did not seek external aid from Russia or Persia, neither was the rebellion a racial war between white and black. In this context Sen wrote:

> For every white soldier in military camps there were certainly twenty black ones, including camp followers, and but for the latter the white troops would have been ineffective. It was the Indian cook who brought the white soldier his dinner under the heaviest fire, and the Indian bhisti who brought him his drink in the thickest of the fight; it was the Indian dooli-bearer who carried the wounded away and the Indian servant who looked after his general comfort ... Of 11,200 effective troops before Delhi, 7,900 were Indians.

In this light we still have to see the real causes of the rebellion in the Company's Bengal Army. Dr Sen says that it began as a military revolt, 'but assumed a political character when the mutineers placed themselves under the King of Delhi (Bahadur Shah, still the Great Mogul in his own right), and a section of the landed aristocracy and the civil population declared in his favour'. True enough, but there must surely have been other causes as well, including religious feelings and protests against foreign rule; here Sen appears very fair to the image of the British raj, in his following comment:

> The Englishman did not deliberately go out of his way to hurt the susceptibilities of the Indian. He had conquered the country by the sword, but he did not want to hold it by the sword alone. He honestly believed that he represented a superior race and a superior culture, and was anxious to share the blessings of Western civilisation with the 'backward' people of the East. He would like to invest his administration with a moral sanction, forgetting that the motives of an alien government are always likely to be misconstrued. Oblivious of the difficulties inherent in his position, he proceeded to introduce reforms which appeared to him unexceptionable ... he did not always discriminate between the essential and the non-essential.

Looking at the broad path of British history in India, before and during the Mutiny, I believe few of our countrymen will not feel able to accept Dr Sen's overall conclusion; we had our share of self-made mistakes, and it would be rash to imagine they did not continue to appear. Furthermore it looks as if political opinion at the East India Company's headquarters in London was never exactly sympathetic to reforms in India. Quotations out of context are sometimes dangerous, but the following passage from an address on the 'Indian Question', delivered by Dr James Burnes at the Court of Proprietors of India Stock, at India House, on 28th January 1858[14], when the Mutiny was far from over, looks very significant. Burnes spent many years in the medical service of the Company:

> A native of India has no notion of political rights, his forefathers had none, and he cannot comprehend their being yielded to him except from a cowardly terror of himself. Such concessions, in fact, are diametrically opposed to his conception of the dignity, and authority of a ruler. What he required from England is a well-chosen, vigorous and benignant Governor-General, armed with ample power to enforce authority, protect person and property, and administer justice promptly and efficiently . . .

Nevertheless, in the purely military sense, the foregoing does not satisfy me, particularly as there were some peculiar conditions facing the Government of India in the decade before the Mutiny. Strange though it may seem, the peace in India that Lord Dalhousie preserved (he was Governor-General 1848-56) was partly the cause of unrest raising its head. In time of war internal troubles generally sleep, but when peace comes men, (particularly in *martial races*) think of their home problems. This may be cynical but it is true! Napoleon and many other famous men in history knew this and acted on it. There were other military factors, particularly the impact of the Crimean War on Whitehall and the draining of British troops from India to Persia and China; astonishingly this left only 45,322 British soldiers in the whole subcontinent with 233,000 Indian troops of the Company's native armies. Between Calcutta and Meerut (all of a thousand miles and excluding Oudh) there were only two British regiments: at Lucknow, and at Dinapore on the Ganges. Worse still, Lord Canning, after he succeeded Dalhousie early in 1857, actually reduced the British troops in Oudh to one weak infantry regiment and one battery of artillery. Finally there was very little cooperation and mutual understanding between the officers of the Company's armies and the British officers in the Civil Service. In my grandfather's papers the first reference to any military matter, professional or social, is in a letter dated 13th January 1845, when James Thomason (then Lieutenant-Governor at Agra) wrote to Robert complaining bitterly about the army in the Punjab. Thomason accused military leaders of obtaining money improperly, by plunder and extortion, and of inaction and lack of offensive spirit.

In all these circumstances it is not difficult to accept the allegations that British officers in Bengal Army regiments were well below standard in all professional business, and generally ignorant of the increasingly dangerous state of affairs in their sepoy ranks. They were apathetic and never dreamt that '*their* sepoys in *their* regiment could even contemplate mutiny'. One possible explanation for this lies in the higher moral values of the British officers compared with their predecessors of the Georgian era in India. In the eighteenth century, when there were so few white women in the subcontinent, the practice of keeping a 'native' mistress was much more widespread, and officers were told about subversive tendencies. The 'sleeping dictionary', and the source 'they're saying in the bazaars' often provided very reliable information. For the Victorians, with high ideals about women and their acceptance of repressed sexual desires outside marriage, the scene changed, and no doubt much worthwhile intelligence was lost. I was impressed by this point when I read it in Bishop Montgomery's handwriting with the annotation: 'Sir Robert said this to me one day when we were discussing the Mutiny.' Clearly sound leadership by officers in most regiments of the Bengal Army did not exist, for so much that could have been done, at regimental level, to prevent the Mutiny went by default. All in all then, the one sound and practical reason for the mutiny was the lack of proper training for the British officers and the failure of the East India Company to enforce it. Field-Marshal Slim's adage 'there are no bad regiments, only bad officers' was as true then as now.

I visited India in 1978 and came away convinced that the educated classes, the men and women who rule India, look on the years 1857-58 as witness to the first faint stirrings of an ideal - indigenous freedom without foreign domination - and, in that sense, the Mutiny in *their* view was inevitable. If we try to look at all that happened, in those years and thereafter, from the standpoint of current Indian nationalism (keeping in mind two World Wars and the vast influence and movements of Mahatma Gandhi and Mohamed Ali Jinnah) we must surely expect them to hold such opinion. I did not visit Pakistan but I feel equally convinced the same view will predominate there. Of course my grandfather and his contemporaries never dreamt there would one day be an end to British rule. Still less did they imagine that the second generation following them (only ninety years after the Mutiny) would see *their* India divided and the British withdraw from the subcontinent, though, as Dr Sen wrote, 'with good grace and undiminished prestige'.

In this book I make no attempt to tell the whole story of the great Mutiny, or describe the many fierce battles that took place; my purpose is to concentrate on those events and controversies in which my grandfather became chiefly concerned, including his time as Chief Commissioner in the troubled province of Oudh.

After the successful disarming at Lahore, Robert Montgomery and his wife and family (their two young sons James and Ferguson, their daughter Lucy, just one year old, and Robert's daughter Mary, now eighteen) continued to live in their house at Anarkulli. Of course it had been, and still was, a dangerous and worrying time for British families in particular, the majority of whom had moved into Lahore Fort where conditions were crowded and very hot. But Robert had refused to leave his home; he was the senior officer in Lahore, he had double sentries of armed Sikh police at his house, where it was very comfortable, and he retained his full retinue of servants, all now Muslim or Sikh. Furthermore they had their horses and were evidently able to ride as usual, but always with mounted escort, never alone. The following letter was written by Robert to his sister Charlotte at Moville, just six weeks after the execution of the 26th Regiment mutineers:

New Park
Anarkulli, Lahore

16th Sept. 1857

My dearest Charlotte,
        Here we are I am thankful to say well and strong and this, in these times, is a great mercy. I believe you get the *Lahore Mail* and you will learn much from it, much that is terrible and very disheartening. India has indeed been suffering, and I wish I could say her troubles were over. Perhaps the *Mail* will take home news of the fall of Delhi, if so, a great step has been gained. If we fail in taking it, it will be a bad business, but I don't anticipate this. The enemy are strong, more numerous than we are, they are all disciplined troops, and behind a wall one man is as good as another. We are anxious about Lucknow, and General Havelock who tried to relieve the garrison was obliged to fall back till he gets reinforcements, and they are not very near. We have been greatly blessed and favoured in the Punjab, we had much in our favour and should be very thankful for it; the murders and atrocities committed were fearful. I am always busy as before, but I cannot say I do much real work. There is constant excitement from perpetually occurring events and it keeps us all in health. At this season, end of monsoon, all are usually prostrated with sickness, yet now there is hardly any with, mercifully, no cholera that is so dreadful. In summer time we always escaped to the hills as a necessary measure; this year if I had wished to go I could not have left my post and the family are all here.
        The future of India is all obscure: but we shall have a firmer hold than ever and God is working His purpose out and for His own ends, tho' we see not how. Poor Dorothea Alexander will have felt deeply Walter's death, there are thousands in this country who can mourn with her, and many only too thankful to hear that their friends are dead, and have not been cruelly mutilated. The attempt to elevate the natives has failed dismally, those most honoured have gone against us. They put me in mind of the Irish proverb, 'Keep them down and they'll lie down, give them a head and off they go'! I trust we may all yet be spared to meet and talk of all the goodness and mercy that has followed us all our lives.

Yours affectionate Brother
R. Montgomery

There is no doubt that Robert's conviction, so clear in this letter to his sister, that God was on the side of the British and would lead them to victory, in His own good time, was fully shared by his contemporaries in the Company's service. Equally clear is the apparent determination to stop the clock of reforms, to dominate the people and 'keep them down'. Gone, apparently, was the will to determine a just and impartial settlement of all issues, between class and race, Hindu and Muslim, for all must now pay the penalty. Was it this new attitude that found expression in cold-blooded cruelties often perpetrated by the British on their mutineers-cum-murderers, with no distinction made between the innocent and the guilty? But it is easy to 'pontificate' and forget the evidence of really appalling atrocities by Muslims and Hindus alike. Englishmen were driven mad by stories of officers murdered, their children butchered and British women raped and then killed; one example is enough. Clifford, Assistant Collector of Gurgaon, heard that in Delhi his sister and her friend Miss Jennings (daughter of the local chaplain) 'were stripped naked by rebels at the King's Palace [the Red Fort], tied to the wheels of gun-carriages, dragged through the Chandni Chauk [the street of the silversmiths so familiar to all of us] and there publicly raped before being cut to pieces'. Small wonder that afterwards, when Delhi fell, Clifford said he had 'put to death all he had come across, not excepting women and children'.

Those are the facts, for both sides, and it is difficult, if not impossible and perhaps wiser not to try, to strike a balance – between right and wrong. Dr Sen took the neutral line, that is easy to accept, when he wrote:

Nor was the war of 1857 a conflict between barbarism and civilisation, for neither side observed a single restriction which humanity had imposed, and which oriental and occidental nations had tacitly agreed to honour. It was an inhuman fight between people driven insane by hatred and fear. The non-combatants suffered as badly at the hands of infuriated soldiery as the men-at-arms. Age and sex offered scanty protection against primitive cruelty, and even death brought no immunity from wanton insult ... Hindu, Muslim and Christian alike relapsed into primitive savagery.

In the event, reconciliation followed some eighteen months later. Queen Victoria proclaimed a general amnesty and forgiveness for all offences by all concerned, and peace, law and order, unity and stability prevailed. Looking back, surely war has always been horrible for 'all concerned'. Can we say with certainty that the atrocities I have cited, by British and Indian, were greater than those of Hitler and the Japanese in World War II? In World War I, British infantry, hard pressed for manpower in the awful trench warfare of France and Flanders, were prone to shoot dead their German prisoners of war who had already surrendered, when they found they had insufficient men to escort 'Huns' back to the rear. In Burma in

1945 the Japanese, in retreat, deliberately killed their own wounded lest any fall into our hands alive.

Just before Christmas 1857 my grandfather wrote a letter to his brother in Ireland, telling him of his life in the Punjab at that time. Delhi had been recaptured but the Mutiny was still far from over.

Lahore

18th Dec. 1857

My dearest brother,

I fear it is not very often I write to you, but I must do so this time. We are all, I am thankful to say, well.

India is still in a very unsettled state, and my old station Cawnpore seems to be the centre of the strife at present. There has been no direct intelligence from there for nearly 4 weeks, though a few days ago a scrap of paper, in Greek characters, was received calling for cavalry reinforcements. The rebels do all they can to prevent our people carrying letters, and a common plan to deceive them is to hide a scrap of paper rolled up in a quill, which is kept in the courier's mouth! I believe the mutineers of the Gwalior contingent advancing on Cawnpore have been beaten and dispersed, but again all posts are cut off and a mail runner can only go about 30 miles a day. We hear all the Lucknow people are safe and communication down the Ganges below Cawnpore is open. It is a mercy we are quiet here; not a single soldier has reached us from England since the outbreak now 7 months ago, and the few we have left in the Punjab are many of them sick and unfit for duty. I do not think we have now anything to fear, but we shall be very glad to see troops coming up via Karachi and Mooltan. The Government will not be firmly established again for at least 6 months, and there will be desultory fighting for a year.

We have decided to send Jamie (James) home with our friends the Raikes, who are very superior people, so Jamie will go on with his lessons as usual till they reach England. You will like Jamie I think the best of all. He is a fine stirring well grown boy, and I think a good boy. He is a splendid rider and takes his gallop with Mary and me every morning. He is the only one of the family with the true Montgomery face. Mary is very well and enjoys above all things her morning rides. We are going into camp after Christmas, and I think she will enjoy the life. From there we shall march to Ferozepore where the Raikes, from Agra, will join us, and then they embark with Jamie to go down the Sutlej and Indus to Karachi. From there they go to Bombay to catch the steamer for Suez. The Raikes have their own family, the youngest 9 years old; they will probably stay at Malta for a short time, then at Geneva, and then on to England the beginning of summer.

Lady (John) Lawrence has started for England, you will like her when you see her. But she is very cold-hearted, cares not a straw for anyone, when out of sight, and is a fare-you-well (Killarney) sort of person!

Yours affectionate brother
R. Montgomery

As will be seen later young James Montgomery was not after all sent home with the Raikes. Conditions in the Punjab worsened, and the long journey by river to the sea might have been very hazardous; by now shallow draught steamers were operating on the Indus as far as Dera Ismail Khan, but above there, and on the Punjab waterways, only slow old country boats were available. Sir John's wife (Harriette Lawrence) was the daughter of the Rev. Richard Hamilton, Rector of Culdaff in Inishowen, and therefore well known to both Robert and Honoria Lawrence (Henry's wife); evidently Robert did not really care for Harriette! The Donegal clergy of those days seemed to have shared two main propensities – sending their children to India and having large families. Harriette's grandfather, the Rev. James Hamilton, married three times and, according to Burke's Peerage of the time, was credited with having had 36 sons and daughters! Local tradition had it the number was 39, to accord with the 39 Articles of the Protestant faith! And Anne Montgomery, Robert's grandmother who died in 1818, had eight children, the last of whom, according to Robert, was born when she was 53!

Jamie (James Alexander Lawrence Montgomery) was seven years old when all the native regiments were disarmed at Lahore. Years later he wrote this note about it:

In 1857 we all remained the whole, dreadfully hot, summer in Anarkulli and my mother refused to tell me why we did not go to Dharmsala. I well recall the day when all the native regiments were disarmed in the nearby cantonment at Mian Mir. My step-sister Mary (then 18, she used to teach us and we liked her very much) had said the night before we should not be going for our usual ride in the morning. I remember it was still dark, for I woke up as the lamps were lit, when a number of senior civil officers came to the house on horseback. Of course I dressed at once and came to ask what was happening, but my mother merely said 'Your father is going to attend an important parade'. But I saw him wearing a sword and buckle on his belt with a revolver under his coat, before mounting his horse and riding away with the others. My mother said 'You'd better go back to bed', but it was getting light so I went into the garden to talk to the *malis* who were already at work.

I could see my mother and Mary were very anxious about something and Mr Henry Perkins, the youngest of the civil officers, remained in the house with us. Then after some hours, it must have been nearly 10 o'clock, my father and his party came riding back. They all looked extremely pleased and sat down to a very good breakfast, which I was allowed to join. I remembered it well because there were all sorts of dishes I didn't normally have for breakfast!

The 'Mutiny' volume of my grandfather's papers shows very clearly the paramount importance he attached, after the successful disarming at Lahore, to keeping the Sikhs of the Punjab on the side of government. He appreciated that if the Sikh Sirdars and their soldiers, raised and trained in the tradition of Ranjit Singh's magnificent army, but twice defeated by the British, should take their revenge by joining the mutineers, the military and political consequences for our rule in India would be disastrous. The news that the redoubtable Sikh army was siding with the rebels (there were nearly 40,000 regular native troops in the province) would spread like wild fire, and be interpreted as a signal, *to millions*, that the Company's raj was finished. In this light the great city of Amritzar appeared vital, for Amritzar is to the Sikhs what Mecca is to the Muslims and Benares to the Hindus; above all Amritzar, forty miles from Lahore, was commanded by the celebrated fortress of Govindgarh, and the latter must remain in safe hands. But a strong detachment from the 59th Bengal Native Infantry was guarding the fort, together with only seventy European artillerymen. Robert Montgomery knew that he must act with speed and decision.

Immediately after that very pleasant breakfast at Anarkulli my grandfather returned to Mian Mir to arrange matters with Brigadier-General Corbett, Lahore Garrison Commander, who co-operated fully. What followed is best told in Robert's own words:

That morning, 13th, Richard Lawrence, Captain of Police, and Roberts, Commissioner of Lahore Division, drove off to Amritzar; they were to make all speed in order to ascertain the state of mind of the 59th at Govindgarh, and also to assure the Sikh Durbar that Government was on their side, and would immediately raise fresh irregular (Sikh) regiments for the army, and take more Sikhs into the Police and government service, and the Levies. It was vital for us to have the loyalty and support of the Maharajah of Patiala, and the Rajas of Jind and Nabha. Meanwhile that same night a Company of the 81st Foot at Lahore set off for Govindgarh in ekkas or native one-horse gigs. The soldiers entered the fortress peacefully at dawn on 14th, and replaced the 59th detachment who withdrew without trouble.

A great deal is left unsaid in that brief record by Robert. Neither the railway nor the Grand Trunk Road had yet reached Lahore and the journey by night of a company of British infantry, still in their thick uniforms (which had not yet been simplified) along the rough country tracks, must have been dreadfully hot, uncomfortable and very tiring. In reality an *ekka* was an ox-cart drawn by a pony, not like the *tonga* of our day or a conventional gig, and more than a hundred were requisitioned to transport the infantry with their arms, ammunition and equipment. What a sight they must have presented, for they had to drive at top speed at night, and woe betide oncoming ox-carts, camels, etc,! They commandeered fresh horses at pre-arranged halts. The British infantryman has always been adaptable and can take most things, and no doubt it was this that made a sergeant of the 81st remark to his commanding officer, when told about the impending trip to Govindgarh: 'It's them niggers at it again, I suppose Sir'! But the greatest achievement was the success of Richard Lawrence and Roberts, the Commissioner, who succeeded so well in retaining the allegiance of the Sikh community. Of course their task was assisted by the way the Sikhs disliked and despised the Hindustani sepoys (the 'poorbeahs') who formed the greater part of the Bengal Army native regiments – they were mostly Brahmans and Rajputs from the Ganges Valley and Muslims from Bihar; the Sikhs were pro-Punjab before all else and had always respected the British. Clearly my grandfather's instant reaction over Amritzar, and the warning he had already sent, on 12th May to the great arsenal at Ferozepore, one of the largest in India, paid immense dividends.

Strangely it was Sir John Lawrence himself who was, at first, so cautious about enlisting Sikhs. On 13th May he sent the following signal to Colonel Macpherson, Military Secretary to the Punjab Government:

By Electric Telegraph
Rawalpindi

13th May 1857

From Captain James
To Colonel Macpherson, Lahore

Be careful not to take any measures towards raising the Sikhs without orders. The Chief Commissioner is averse to the measure *without reference to government*. Glad tò hear of the Mian Mir doings going off *so quietly*.

(sd) H. R. James
Offg. Secy. to Chief
Commissioner, Punjab

Of course by the time this telegram reached Lahore it was too late to act on it! Richard Lawrence and Roberts had already gone to Amritzar on their mission to the Sikh Durbar, and certainly my grandfather made no attempt to stop them! Maybe for this reason he endorsed his copy of the telegram with: 'The words underlined are added to the original draft, in John Lawrence's own handwriting.'

My grandfather evidently protested to Sir John about Sikhs, for on 15th May the latter telegraphed again to Lahore, agreeing to recruitment without qualification.

Chief Commissioner to R. Montgomery, Esq.

Your letter of 14th received – Any men whom you and Macpherson think necessary you may raise.

66

Small wonder Robert kept the original copy of this signal, as received at Lahore, on its blue notepaper endorsed '16 words'!

At this time too another of the great Mutiny characters figures prominently in my grandfather's papers. This was Hodson of Hodson's Horse; a strange man, ruthless, aggressive, rude and very unpopular! Yet he became famous, if only for the fact that he personally arrested Bahadur Shah, the last of the great Moguls, and then shot and killed his three sons 'to remove any question of heirs'. On 20th May Hodson telegraphed to Robert from Kurnal in the Punjab. He was a lieutenant and he certainly had no qualms in his approach to the Judicial Commissioner!

From Lt. Hodson to R. Montgomery, Esq.
Judicial Commissioner

I have been ordered to raise a Regt. of Irregular Horse and have been appointed as Comdt. Pray send to Kurnal any good men you can get for me - Sikhs especially. The duty is urgent, we will have no horses whatever here of our own. I am sure you will aid me. I wrote to you asking for Kunsingh Rosah, pray send him. Could you get permission for some of the Guides to join me - volunteers of course. Any promise as to pay and promotion you make will be carried out.

Unfortunately there is no record of Robert's reply; but I feel sure he helped Hodson all he could because in my family that was always our understanding, and I remember Bishop Montgomery saying, 'that Sir Robert was the founder of Hodson's Horse'. In those far off days cavalrymen were enlisted on the *silladari* system, under which a recruit undertook to join his regiment on the condition that be brought with him his own horse, fit and well trained, with saddlery; when he left the regiment he could sell both to the Sirkar, and if he did not own a horse in the first place he could obtain a loan for its purchase. Hence Hodson's plea that there were no horses available in Kurnal. Hodson's Horse is now a distinguished armoured regiment of the Indian Army.

Three days later John Lawrence wrote to Robert expressing his distrust of Hodson:

23rd May

My dear Robert

Hodson is an officer of tried courage and great capability, but a *mauvais sujet* after all. I am glad we are not to have him. Help him by all means, but too many men raised by an influential man, if for permanent service, are not good.

Later on, however, Lawrence appears to change his attitude, because, according to Bosworth Smith:[15] 'Lawrence allowed Montgomery to raise some men for Hodson at Lahore, and to send them down to Delhi, where they formed the nucleus of the renowned Hodson's Horse.'

A few days later Lawrence wrote again to Robert urging him: 'Pray resist all reaction, all returns of tenderness and sympathy for the mutineers . . .' He need not have worried for Robert's reaction (he had in fact already reacted) was to send the following instruction to all Commissioners and Deputy Commissioners: 'Make over the mutineers to the civil authorities. Should they resist you will of course be prepared to fire on them and destroy them to a man if possible.'

Two quite distinct but entirely different characters appear now in my grandfather's image. Generally he was regarded as a devout and humble Christian, a gentle and kind person; John Lawrence once said 'he was gentle as a lamb'. But see now the difference immediately above! It is a fact that at the taking of Delhi, Robert Montgomery strongly advocated the total destruction of the Jama Musjid, that famous and beautiful mosque, still one of the finest in all India and Pakistan, facing the Red Fort. Looking back one shudders to think what might have been the effect on Muslim thought and opinion of the British, in all India and in the Muslim world generally, if that sacred and beautiful building had been deliberately destroyed! Be that as it may, after the Mutiny one old and distinguished Muslim in the Punjab said: 'John Lawrence was a lion man. Montgomery was an angel man.'

On this question of the possible destruction of Delhi, I found a personal letter to my grandfather from Robert Napier (later Field-Marshal Lord Napier of Magdala) which shows the latter held equally strong views. The letter is dated 30th November 1857 and ends with these words:

> I am very sorry that the walls of Delhi have been spared. The place ought to have been quite laid open, and I hope will be so, as soon as *you* have leisure.
>
> Salaam Bahut
> Yours sincerely
> R. Napier

On the east side of the city wall of Delhi is the wall of the Red Fort (the King's Palace). It is perhaps fortunate that these two men (Robert Napier and Robert Montgomery) were not allowed to destroy both the Jama Musjid and the Red Fort! In the Crypt of St. Paul's Cathedral the memorial plaque to Sir Robert is next to the plaque (and the tomb) of Lord Napier. Would the epitaph on each plaque be the same if both men had had their way at Delhi in 1857?

6
Delhi

As the long hot summer of 1857 dragged on it became increasingly clear to Sir John Lawrence, and his Punjab team, that a military and political victory over the mutineers was not possible until Delhi, the historic capital of India, had been recaptured. The city had been taken on May 11th, and still represented the hard core of rebel resistance, based on a determination to restore Bahadur Shah to the throne as King of Delhi and Emperor of all Hindustan. Meanwhile rebel troops still controlled large areas of Bengal, Bihar, the vast North-Western Provinces, Rohilkand, and particularly Oudh, where Lucknow, its capital city, second only in importance to Delhi, was surrounded and beseiged during June. Particularly unfortunate was the large-scale disruption of communications, so that Lord Canning, the Governor-General, could not leave Calcutta to influence the course of events, including the reinforcement measures that were essential for a successful attack on the rebel positions at Delhi. The mutineers there held large supplies of arms and munitions seized from the arsenal, where the powder magazine had been blown up, but the ordnance depot remained intact. Sir John Lawrence was thus left virtually without any direction from higher authority in his efforts to retake Delhi, which was part of the Punjab and therefore within his jurisdication.

Against this background it is not difficult to appreciate the high tide of activity that engulfed all officials in the Punjab, from the first day of the Mutiny until its final ending. Furthermore, although the disarming at Lahore and the continued loyalty of the greater part of the Sikh population, and the Sikh Princes, ensured that the province did not come under rebel control, there were nevertheless twelve mutinies in the Punjab (by regular cavalry or infantry garrisons) that had to be ruthlessly suppressed. John Lawrence's military commitments were therefore very

69

considerable, including the fact that, with some exceptions, the regular units of the Bengal Army could no longer be entirely trusted; the raising of new regiments, particularly irregular units, was a first priority and a very urgent one. Irregular regiments (so called) differed from their regular counterparts only by the terms of their enlistment, their lack of insistence on formal military routine and turn out, never of discipline, and, in particular, because each unit generally had only three British officers - a vital distinction as regular Bengal infantry battalions had twenty-three British officers. A brief recital of the military events in the Punjab, with which my grandfather was so closely involved, is essential to this story.

Eighteen new infantry regiments and 7000 irregular cavalry were raised in the province, making an army of 34,000 men, mainly Sikhs and Punjabi Muslims. 'These totals,' Robert added, 'included sixteen Christians.' He himself raised five troops of Irregular cavalry and sent them to Hodson's Horse at Kurnal. I found a note about this recently, in Bishop Montgomery's handwriting. The Punjab Irregular Frontier Force ('The Piffers'), of five cavalry regiments, nine infantry battalions, with four mountain batteries of artillery, formed the major part of this newly-raised Punjab army, and included The Guides. Many famous men served with The Piffers during the Mutiny, some of them recognised to this day in regular Indian and Pakistan Army regimental titles: Coke, Lumsden, Wilde, Daly, Probyn, Watson, John Nicholson, Rothney, Renny, Henderson, Hughes, Kennedy and Younghusband. The Frontier Force was a civil armed contingent, not under the army Commander-in-Chief, though raised and trained by British military officers and then (with its officers) placed wholly under the orders of the Chief Commissioner of the Province. Its exact counterpart, of our day, were The Scouts and The Militias (The Tochi, Kurram, South Waziristan, Chitral, The Zhob, etc.) who operated in the tribal territory of the North-West Frontier Province and were formally named the Civil Armed Forces, or CAF.

Unfortunately it was not until 6th June that the Delhi (Relief) Field Force, at that time its total strength barely exceeded 4000, fought its way to within two miles of the city and encamped on the famous 'Ridge', north west of the Kashmir Gate. The Ridge was the site of the military cantonment where six battalions of Bengal Native Infantry, but no British troops, had been in garrison on 11th May - I shall revert later to the events of that awful day and how my grandfather became involved in the conduct of the seige. The background was the walled city itself, seven miles in circumference and flanked on the east by the Jumna River, but completely open on its south and west faces but for the small force on The Ridge. Delhi was thus a very formidable fortress, with its city population of 150,000 and a well-armed garrison that greatly outnumbered the Field Force, particularly in heavy artillery; the rebels had five times as many guns, all well served and with plenty of ammunition. During the entire three and a half months of the siege – ironically it was the Field Force that was beseiged as much as the walled city – mutineers were reinforcing or deserting from the rebel army, via the two open flanks, virtually as they pleased.

The low professional standard of the senior military commanders was almost the worst of Sir John's problems. The Commander-in-Chief, General Anson, was sixty, not in good health and in the hills for the hot weather when the Mutiny broke out at Meerut. Lord Canning immediately telegraphed to him: 'Act at once and retake Delhi.' But Anson was slow and inactive, and did not reach Ambala, 140 miles from Delhi, till 16th May, by which time the mutineers in the city had consolidated their position. General Anson, as a professional soldier, took the view that 'he could not allow himself to be hurried by an impatient civilian, whose ignorance led him to underestimate military difficulties and the political consequences of another disaster.' Not surprisingly perhaps, more troubles followed. Anson died of cholera on 25th May and was succeeded by General Sir Henry Barnard, a Crimea War veteran and new to India; he too was of advanced years and also died of cholera, on 5th July. General Reed then became commander of the Field Force, but he was a chronic invalid, 'fit for little more than lying on his bed all day',[16] and resigned his appointment on 14th July.

However, even worse followed, for Reed's successor was Brigadier-General Wilson, the station commander at Meerut on 10th May, where he became forever famous for his inaction and lack of drive and daring; then, to cap all, General Hewitt, who was the senior officer at Meerut, was still the divisional commander and therefore has overall command of troops and operations in the Delhi area. Hewitt was nearly seventy and had been first commissioned in the Bengal Native Infantry in 1806; he was 'finished' in any professional military context.

Four clearly unsuitable and inadequate holders of the key military appointments, within less than seven weeks, was an extraordinary situation. Small wonder that Sir John Lawrence wrote to Robert about it, almost in despair.

2 July 1857
Nr. Pindee

My dear Robert

I have written to the Nawab of Bahawalpore to look after his people, but until we take Delhi it is not much good my threatening, it may well do harm. I wish you and I had the hanging of old Hewitt, we could hang him up with much gusto. Is it not wretched to think that such a man is entrusted with vital interests: I feel horribly disgusted. How is all this to end? Even if we do well and retake Delhi it will require years to redeem the last six weeks. We shall be very hard up for money. Keep all the common levies (additional Police) as low as you can manage. Funds are not to be got in sufficient quantities in Calcutta. As for Bombay they have none. There must be a bankruptcy unless England comes forward.

Yours affectionately
John Lawrence

Meanwhile the military situation, despite the unfortunate delay and lack of leadership at the top, was developing with the aim, first and foremost, of reinforcing the Delhi Field Force, though without prejudice to maintaining internal security in every district of the Punjab - the only province from which reinforcements could be found. A Mobile Column, commanded in the first place by Neville Chamberlain, had been formed at Peshawar and ordered to Delhi. It was then that The Guides made their historic march, ahead of the Column, direct from their headquarters at Mardan to the Delhi Ridge, 580 miles, in 22 days, in the hottest season of the year. When the regiment reached the Ridge on the morning of 9th June they were asked how soon they could be ready to attack; they replied 'In half an hour'. They did, and lost all their officers, killed or wounded.

In his papers my grandfather always referred to the 'Mobile Column', but most writers have called it 'The Movable Column'; but whichever adjective is used the Column was certainly an *ad hoc* and rapidly raised assortment of units, recruited mainly by Edwardes, Commissioner of Peshawar Division, and trained by Captain John Nicholson. The latter was an Irishman, born in Dublin but brought up in Ulster by his mother, who belonged to the Hogg family and were settlers from Scotland like the Lawrences and Montgomerys. Young Nicholson was educated at the Royal School at Dungannon in Co. Tyrone, and owed the start of his career to his uncle, James Hogg, who had made a fortune in India and was a director of the East India Company.

Of all the famous British officers who, as it were, march across the pages of every history book on the Indian Mutiny, Nicholson is second to none in his distinction and high reputation. Some twelve years younger than my grandfather he was commissioned in the Bengal Native Infantry (he did not go to Addiscombe) and joined his regiment at the age of seventeen. He took part in the disastrous first Afghan War in which, like George Lawrence, he became a prisoner of the Afghans, after which he was seconded to the Civil Service as a Deputy Commissioner in the Peshawar Division. In appearance he was tall, broad-shouldered and robust with dark hair and eyes, very attractive to women, though taciturn and not given to social life in any way. He was always a stern and ruthless disciplinarian, essentially a soldier who acted always with determination and speed. On horseback, armed only with a sword, he hunted and killed tiger, a truly daring and astonishing exploit that probably accounted in large measure for his adoption as a God by a sect of devout but martial Hindus. They believed and declared that *Jan Nikal Seyn* was the reincarnation of Brahma, the God of Creation. However Nicholson, who was a strong churchman of the traditional Protestant school of Ulstermen, utterly rejected any such notion about himself, and regarded it as tantamount to blasphemy. When therefore his *Nikalseynis* came to worship him in camp he took immediate disciplinary action and had them all flogged! But that only increased their devotion, and their belief that 'he punishes us for our own good'; whereupon they were all flogged again!

The Mobile Column began its march to Delhi on 12th June, but inevitably its progress was slow, for the mutinies of the Hindustani regiments, referred to earlier in this chapter, compelled diversion of the Column to disarm and suppress the sepoy garrisons, principally at Jullundur, Phillour, Sialkot, Jhelum and Ferozepore. No other troops were available for these tasks which took a long time to complete and would have certainly taken much longer had not John Nicholson assumed command of the Column at Jullundur on 21st June. The Chief Commissioner had promoted him from Captain to Brigadier-General in one day, which must surely be a record. The famous, and often told, exploits of the Mobile Column during its long march, are no part of this story, except for the involvment of my grandfather in the business. The Column did not reach the Delhi Ridge until the second half of August, though Nicholson went ahead and got there himself on 7th August. The supporting siege train of elephant batteries, of heavy artillery and ammunition, with large quantities of gunpowder and explosives from the great arsenal at Ferozepore, and bridging equipment and tackle (for crossing the moat and scaling walls), and other bulky stores, did not arrive until 4th September.

For the whole period that the Mobile Column was moving through the Punjab, Robert Montgomery was responsible for its safe conduct, that adequate police escorts, particularly for the ponderous siege train, were found, and that village headmen and local chiefs were not slow in providing labour or transport when requisitioned by the military. This part of the task was made easier by the knowledge that if any local authority was backward in providing assistance then John Nicholson would use force to get what he wanted. Robert certainly informed all his subordinates accordingly, adding his personal approval. But there was far more to it than just administrative assistance; the whole province had to be kept quiet and undisturbed to ensure maximum effort was available in retaking Delhi. This meant keeping absolute control of all the numerous ferries and passages over the Punjab rivers, complete censorship of all mail wherever and whenever thought necessary, safe custody of all treasure and money supplies, and stringent action with criminals. As Judicial Commissioner, Robert issued an edict that any two British officials could sentence to death any person who broke the law, and then carry out the order. Finally, the civil courts had to remain open and all revenue due to Government had to be paid; it was vital to keep all children's schools open, and this was done.

One of the best descriptions of the state of affairs in the province at this time, with which Robert had to cope, is provided by Dr Sen who wrote:

> How little the British rulers could depend on the affection of the Punjab villages. Arson, murder, highway robbery, cattle lifting, and decoity suddenly revived; and some of the offenders, when apprehended, naively accounted for their misconduct by confessing 'that they believed the rule of the British to be over'.

Looking again at my last two paragraphs my grandfather's measures appear as instruments of exceptionally strict martial law, but if the Column and the siege train were ever to reach Delhi they were essential measures, particularly when viewed against the Column's own difficulties. Many of the soldiers recruited by Edwardes were warlike Pathans from territory between the Indus and the Afghan frontier, who spoke only Pushtu, and were never without weapons in their daily lives: Afghans, Afridis, Orakzais, Yusufzais, Wazirs, Mahsuds. They knew only tribal law and discipline and now had to learn military drill and practice, in days rather than weeks. They were horsemen but there were never enough horses, even for the horse artillery, and most had to march on foot, or travel in *ekkas*, or *tongas*, or any kind of horse-drawn vehicle; and of course there was the transport echelon for equipment and ammunition, including the camp followers and baggage, all loads being conveyed on pack ponies or mules. The much slower siege train, with its very heavy loads, relied for transportation on elephants, camels and ox-carts and required strong armed escorts. What a wonderful sight the siege train must have been, with elephants drawing guns and carrying very heavy loads, and scores of camels, both riding and baggage animals, as well as hundreds of ox-carts; all very vulnerable to sudden armed robbery, arson, plain theft or any transport breakdown, day and night. Robert noted that near Sialkot Nicholson wanted 100 additional *ekkas*, but the local headman refused them. Nicholson said: 'Shoot him at once unless he produces them.' He did!

Climatic conditions also posed great problems for the Mobile Column and the siege train. The monsoon season was just beginning and there were days of immense heat with merciless sunshine, alternated with dreadful humidity when low clouds, and the dust in the atmosphere, totally obscured the sun. Then came the rains, with tremendous thunderstorms, causing the wheels of guns and their limbers to sink to their axles at ferry crossings or on swamp ground. Disease and fatigue also took their toll, and there was little sleep, with virtually no rest for all ranks, because Nicholson was for ever urging them on. When, for once, there was an opportunity to halt for a night and allow the officers of the Column to dine in a civilised fashion, they took it. However, about half-way through the meal Nicholson suddenly appeared. 'Gentlemen, I do not want you to hurry your dinner, but the Column marches in half an hour'![17]

All through June and July, John Lawrence was obsessed with the need to send more and more troop reinforcements to Delhi, at the expense of the remaining garrisons in the Punjab. On 19th July General Wilson informed the Chief Commissioner that without reinforcements he could not hold out much longer on the Ridge, in the face of repeated rebel assaults from the city. 'When will the Movable Column and siege train arrive? Can you not help us now?' This was the message that reached Lawrence at Lahore where he had arrived for a fleeting visit. It was then that Sir John sent an additional 4000 troops (taken from the Frontier Force, with one British regiment) direct to the Ridge, thereby reducing the British element of the Punjab garrisons, including the frontier defence, to 5600 men; otherwise in the province there were 18,000 Hindustani troops, few of them still armed and all of doubtful loyalty - a very dangerous situation. In these cirumstances Lawrence was prepared to pay an awful, and indeed astonishing, price in order to ensure the recapture of Delhi. This was no less than a proposal to abandon Peshawar, so that all troops engaged on border defence could be withdrawn behind the Indus, and thus allow him to divert more troops and military resources for a final assault on Delhi.

Sir John had long held this view, for as early as mid-June he had sent this personal letter to my grandfather. His handwriting was always atrocious and sometimes quite illegible.

Private and Confidential

Nr. Pindee

17th June 1857

Mr dear Monty

I send you a copy of a letter I have sent to Edwardes. It was not intended to copy all of it, but the point I want you and Donald Mcleod [Financial Commissioner] to consider, and give me your opinion is regarding Peshawar. God forbid that any disaster should occur at Delhi, still it may be His Will, and in that case the question is how we are best to meet the storm that will break over us. James [Military Secretary to the Chief Commissioner] is very averse to my plea of giving up Peshawar, and says we can hold it. I don't think we can; and fear that in making the attempt we shall ruin ourselves. If we retire before we have too, while our Europeans [troops] are in health and strength, we can do it without much difficulty. But in September and

October, if we can meantime hold out so long, they will all be prostrate with fever [after the hot weather and monsoon], and could offer no effective resistance.

I myself do not see the great value of Peshawar. The cost of maintenance is very large. Its only advantage is that in the event of an invasion by a Russo-Persian army, we could more advantageously meet the invaders at the mouth of the Passes than after they had [regrouped?] themselves in the Valley. But the giving up of Peshawar will not prevent them doing this in the event of an invasion, more particularly if it were in the possession of an Ally.[18]

James seems to think that if we give up Peshawar and Kohat, which is what I propose, that the Punjab must follow. But this I do not perceive; and even should it be the case, I would relinquish the latter [Punjab] without regret to consolidate ourselves in India.

We must recollect that we cannot expect reinforcements to arrive at Calcutta from England until October, and up here before November or December. And even if we are alive by that time, what a state we shall be in. Half India will have to be reconquered.

Yours affectly
John Lawrence

Clearly the Chief Commissioner was fearful of the dire results that would follow if the small army on the Ridge were defeated, and had to retreat *back into the Punjab*. In that case all the country between the Jumna and the Sutlej rivers would rise against the British, and, worse still, the loyalty of the Sikhs would be strained to breaking point, with catastrophic results throughout the Punjab. He held strongly that the natives of India, different in habits, character, languages colour and religions from their British masters, would *everywhere* rise against the *foreign ruler*, if they saw the latter defeated and in retreat from Delhi, the historic capital of their country. He was therefore prepared, if necessary, to ask Dost Mohammad, the ruler of Afghanistan, to occupy Peshawar, on the understanding that if he did not side with the mutineers Peshawar should remain Afghan territory after the rebellion had been suppressed. Sir John argued that Peshawar (before the first Afghan War) had recently belonged to the Afghans and that its reversion to them would ensure their permanent friendship. Above all he stipulated that a British withdrawal to Attock, at the Indus, would free sufficient troops to ensure the recapture of Delhi, which, for him, meant the safety of India.

Looking back, after nearly a century and a quarter, at Sir John Lawrence's dilemma we must surely credit him with the breadth of vision to plan for what he saw as a likely event - a British retreat from Delhi. But all the senior officers in the Punjab whom he consulted, rejected and were indeed horrified by his proposal, which they regarded as the prime recipe for disaster in all India. They realised that when Sir John spoke of 'giving up Peshawar', he did not mean just the Peshawar Valley and the Khyber

The family portraits at the home of
Field Marshall Montgomery in
Hampshire, showing left to right:
Field Marshall Montgomery, Bishop
Montgomery, Sir Robert Montgo-
mery, Rev. Samuel Montgomery,
and another portrait of the Field
Marshall by James Gunn, the only
portrait of him wearing *one* medal
ribbon (the American D.S.M.)

Sir Robert Montgomery in his old
age, *c*.1885.

Family group at New Park c.1882,
five years before Sir Robert died. He
is seen holding his grandchild, the
daughter of Bishop Montgomery
(who is at the left of the front row).
His wife is sitting on the ground,
one of his sisters is next to him and
the other is on the far right.

Sir Robert Montgomery's famous
camel carriage at Lahore c.1860.

The Punjab's executive council in 1857. Sir John is in the centre with Sir Robert on his left. Sir John was made a peer in 1869, the only viceroy not to be a peer before he was appointed.

An original portrait of Sir John Lawrence c.1856.

Captain Richard Lawrence, Chief of Police at Lahore in 1857 where the Mutiny erupted. He provided Sir Robert with essential intelligence of the impending Mutiny.

This illustration depicting Sir Robert's visit to Kashmir was published in *The Illustrated London News* on 5th September 1863. Sir Robert and Lady Montgomery made the journey to visit Maharajah Runbir Singh, with their large retinue and their state elephants, from Pathankot over the 9000-foot high Banihal Pass into the Vale of Kashmir, with its luxuriant flowers and gardens, watered by the Jhelvim River.

Montgomery Hall, Lahore, built in memory of Sir Robert by the princes and people of the Punjab after he had left India in 1865. Subsequently the hall became the Lahore Gymkhana Club. In the background is the Lawrence Hall.

Captain Heyland, A D C to Sir Robert when the latter was Lt. Governor of the Punjab from 1859 to 1865. He was a professional soldier in the Bengal Army of the East India Company, and was noted for his good looks.

Sir Henry Lawrence *c*.1856.

Colonel Reynall Taylor, during the siege of Delhi in 1857. He had raised the Guides at Mardan. He was a 'Godly' man but also a noted swordsman, renowned for his skill in hand-to-hand combat on the frontier.

The scene at Lahore on the occassion of the great Durbar held in October 1864 when the Viceroy came back to the Punjab.

Sir Robert at Simla in 1856 with his daughter Mary Susan by his first wife. This daughter married Major Crofton of the Bengal Engineers and died in 1860. Simla was the first hill station built by the Raj.

Sir Robert Montgomery's bust in
the India Office.

Lady Ellen Jane Montgomery in
India in 1854.

Pass. Contemporary history on this matter, particularly by the great historians of the nineteenth century like Sir John Kaye, referred only to Sir John's proposal 'to abandon Peshawar and retire to Attock and the Indus, thus setting free some 3000 European troops for Delhi'. I believe that the most explicit definition of his proposal that John Lawrence ever gave is in the above quoted letter (in his own handwriting) to Robert Montgomery, with its reference to 'if we give up Peshawar *and* Kohat, which is what I propose . . .' Of course in those days there was no 'Durand Line' to define the geographical frontier with Afghanistan – that did not come until 1894. Instead there was a vast trans-Indus tribal territory, wild and mountainous, exceeding 40,000 square miles and reaching down south to Sind and Baluchistan, over which the Raj had official, yet not administrative, control; but it was all part of the Punjab, and from it Sir John proposed the British should withdraw their presence completely. This huge tract included the historic mountain passes (the Khyber, Kurram, Tochi, Gomal) over which Alexander the Great, followed by all the Muslim conquerors since Mahmud of Ghazni in the eleventh century, had poured into India. The Derajat, all North and South Waziristan, and beyond the Kurram and Khyber into Dir and Swat, and the Ambela Pass where later Robert Montgomery was to be responsible for a frontier campaign, all this would have been surrendered to Afghan rule.

In the event fate intervened to rescue the Chief Commissioner from the necessity to make this decision; for on 1st August the small army on the Ridge won a gallant victory over a determined rebel assault from the city, thus giving some much needed respite until Nicholson's Column arrived. Ironically, Lord Canning had sent a telegram, signed on 10th July, to Sir John that read: 'Hold on to Peshawar to the last'. However, as we have seen, communications with Calcutta were so bad that Canning's signal had actually been sent by sea to Madras, and thence to Bombay, from where it did not reach Lawrence at Rawalpindi until 7th August.

Robert Montgomery had been as adamant as Edwardes, James (his Military Secretary), General Cotton, commanding the troops at Peshawar, and of course John Nicholson, in urging the Chief Commissioner to drop his proposal to withdraw to the Indus. Indeed it was the civil departments of the Punjab Government, represented by Robert, which drew attention to the very adverse consequences for the sepoy ranks that must follow any large scale abdication of territorial responsibility. So many Pathan tribesmen had been recruited into Punjab regiments, particularly in Piffer units, all of whom had families and relatives trans-Indus; the knowledge, or even mere rumour, that the British were about to hand over their tribal tracts to the Afghans, would have had an immediate and drastic effect on their morale, and raised fears for the safety of their families, *and their pensions*. These fears would have been widespread, at the very time when

Nicholson's Column, and the seige train, were on their long march to Delhi, during which the Column in particular had to fight several fierce and arduous engagements; the cumulative effect on the sepoy ranks would have been crucial.

I have written at length about Sir John Lawrence's withdrawal proposal because it was the only occasion, in his long and close association with my grandfather, that the two men disagreed on policy. Also, in my research, I have not seen the real, likely, effects of the proposed retirement set out in any detail, not even in Bosworth Smith's *Life of Lord Lawrence*. Personally I believe not many British officers who served in India before Independence would doubt that the withdrawal John Lawrence contemplated would probably, if implemented, have brought about the end ot British rule in the subcontinent long before it happened a century later. The course of history in Asia, certainly of British history, would have changed. It seems extraordinary that a man of Lawrence's record, revered and respected world wide, should not have appreciated that the Afghans would never under any circumstances have agreed to return the territory he proposed to cede back to them. Furthermore the Mutiny, with Muslim Afghanistan reaching to the frontiers of Sind and Baluchistan, would have been well placed to spread into the Company's Bombay Army, and our prestige would have vanished; maybe the Russian invasion of the North-West Frontier Province, so long the bugbear of our Victorian ancestors, would have actually taken place.

Strangely perhaps, Indian writers so far seem to have written very little about this affair. Dr Sen, in his chapter on the Delhi siege, gave it only one paragraph when he said:

> When the Empire seemed almost lost Lawrence was prepared to pay the highest possible price to keep it. He seriously proposed that Peshawar should be abandoned, the troops engaged on the Frontier should be diverted to India, and Dost Mohammad should be invited to take charge of what once belonged to him. But . . . Lawrence was not called upon to make this supreme sacrifice.

Sen does not actually commit himself to a final conclusion. But Philip Mason, in his *A Matter of Honour* does, for he wrote:

> John Lawrence saw the importance of retaking Delhi . . . He knew he must pay a price for that effort. He was even, to the horror of his faithful disciples, ready to give Peshawar to the Afghans if it would release men for Delhi. He did not take long to make up his mind that he would not hold back British troops from Delhi merely to watch sepoy battalions who might mutiny.

There then is the opposite view that diminished the value of the Punjab province as the only secure and firm military base for the recapture of

Delhi, and disparages the value and exploits of Nicholson's Mobile Column which suppressed many sepoy mutinies on its long march to the capital. I have set out the two opinions on which readers may care to judge. I should add that one senior army officer did support Sir John's proposal. This was the Adjutant General, Sir Neville Chamberlain; he was a Piffer and first commander of the Mobile Column.

I never cease to be amazed at the number and scope of the letters by well-known Mutiny characters, all signed personally by their originators, that my grandfather collected; altogether in his papers there are hundreds, most of them very difficult to read, with cross writing, and some in beautifully clear script. The majority are from Sir John Lawrence to Robert, but there are also the original letters, not copies, that Robert himself sent to his subordinates (he must have demanded to have them back!), and some that his own officers wrote direct to John Lawrence and other officials, again the originals not copies. No doubt my grandfather exercised his discretion when the mail for the Chief Commissioner, addressed to Sir John, arrived at Lahore! We know Robert kept Sir John's letter to him, already quoted, which ended: 'My letters will come addressed to me. When you like you may open them'!

Though this book is by no means an anthology of letters, I have included the following as none of them have been published, and they illustrate my grandfather's life and work at Lahore from May to September 1857.

To Marsden (Bengal Army officer, seconded as Civil Officer at Ferozepore)
From Robert Montgomery

6a.m. Sunday 17th May

My dear Marsden,

I have received you letter, without date, telling me of your chase after the 45th N.I. I doubt not but that none of them will escape. Pray write most urgently to the Raja of Patiala and other Sirdars of native states to secure them.

I have written to General Innes to act at once against the mutineers in Cantonments, to march them off to jail and to be prepared to fire on them. If the General decides on this, which I doubt not he will, you will empty your jail [at Ferozepore].

I almost hope the mutineers will resist. We want an example, and the effect of their destruction will be immense. We have been shilly shallying when men should be blown from guns. Our Empire in India depends on our vigour now. Raise whatever men you require, but act discreetly and keep me daily informed; your letters will all be passed on to Sir John. We anxiously await the result of what is done after your receipt of this dispatch.

Yours sincerely
Robert Montgomery

There had been a mutiny at Ferozepore, where sepoys of the 45th eventually found their way to Delhi. Marsden was regarded as weak.

Letter from Douglas Forsyth, Deputy Commissioner, Ambala.

22nd May 1857

Dear Mr Montgomery

We are sending off troops as fast as we can. But Col. Thomson of the Commissariat has declined all responsibility for forwarding supplies, so the whole arrangements fall on me. We are getting on tolerably well and supplies will be to the fore. But I must crave your leniency regarding all ordinary District work for I have to do everything myself; all my assistants are away and I have 2,500 civil cases unheard.

Yesterday I sent off 2 companies of the 5th N.I. to Roopore as the [local?] people have risen and taken possession of the Hill Forts there, and threaten to attack. The Simla panic was a most unfortunate affair and ladies have suffered severe trials and hardships – my wife amongst the rest. Now all are congregated at Kassowlie, which is fortified and garrisoned by Europeans.

Yours sincerely
Douglas Forsyth

There had been an unfortunate loss of morale at the well known hill station at Simla, where many British officers with their wives, families and friends were spending the hot weather. Rumours started that a Gurkha battalion at Jutogh, nearby, had mutinied and was marching on Simla. An unseemly panic ensued and there was much disorder, and days of confusion – all unnecessary as the rumour was false. Much later Robert's son, James, married Sir Douglas Forsyth's daughter.

In the last week of May, George Barnes, Divisional Commissioner of the Cis-Sutlej States, wrote an important letter to my grandfather. The manuscript is very difficult with cross writing, but he is obviously impatient with the indecision of the military authorities, and the effect on the march of the seige train.

25th May 1857

My dear Montgomery

You must not think that the delay in the movements of the army is owing to any fault on our part. I assure you that carriage and supplies in attendance were promptly procured. The truth is that the C. in C. will not move upon Delhi until he has a siege train, and until he can exchange one battery of Horse Artillery guns for nine-pounders. All this heavy ordnance has to come from Phillour, and at least twenty contradictory orders about it have been sent there. It is at last on its way with an escort provided by ... Chiefs, and was today (25th) at Sirhind. It cannot well be at Kurnal before the 1st June, and the C. in C. decidedly will not move, notwithstanding my most earnest protestations, without it. All his staff talk of the responsibility resting on this little body of Europeans [the staff, sic!] and say it is very well to urge, but it would be reckless to go without complete equipment. I assure you we have provided every thing we were ever asked for.

Yours sincerely
G. Barnes

Presumably George Barnes, he was a very senior officer, did not know that the C-in-C (General Anson) died the day he wrote this letter! Afterwards delays grew worse and, as stated earlier, the siege train did not arrive before Delhi until 4th September.

Two days later Sir John wrote to Robert with his own recommendations for a successor to Anson.

Nr. Pindee

27th May 1857

My dear Monty
Poor Anson you will see is gone. *Entre nous*, I have suggested to the G.G. to call Patrick Grant round from Madras. Henry (my brother) would do still better than Grant, but it would look like a fix!

Yours affectly
John Lawrence

Lieutenant-General Sir Patrick Grant was C-in-C Madras Army, and by then Henry Lawrence was at Lucknow. But either would have brought such changes to the military scene; though would John and Henry Lawrence have worked well together bearing in mind their fracas at Lahore?

The following letter, written early in June by a junior army officer seconded as Deputy Commissioner of a remote Punjab district bordering the North Western Provinces, is typical of so many reports recorded by Robert at Lahore.

From Lt. A.W. Elphinstone, Deputy Commissioner Goagaira
To Robert Montgomery, Esq., Judicial Commissioner, Lahore

Goagaria

2nd June 1857

Sir
All the Ferries over the Sutlej, with the exception of two, have been closed by me. I have no means of guarding effectively the numerous ferries with the Police Force at my command. I therefore sank all the boats at once in low

water thereby interrupting all communications, except at two points where strong detachments have been posted, and any disarmed men (sepoys) will be prevented most effectively from crossing the river. The whole country on either side of the Sutlej is so disorganised that in my view any communication between the two banks should not take place. The submerged boats could be raised without much difficulty, after tranquility has been restored.

At Sirsa the town has been plundered and the whole district is in a state of anarchy. Captain Robertson and his family are believed to have escaped. All the other Europeans at Sirsa, including Captain Hilliard, his wife, children, and brother-in-law have been murdered, and the Europeans at Hansi and Hissar are said also to have been murdered. I have only to add in conclusion that the tranquility of this district will not be affected by the disturbed state of affairs on the other side of the Sutlej.

A.W. Elphinstone

In the event many months passed before Lt. Elphinstone saw his 'Tranquility restored'!

Against the background of this chapter so far, descriptive of murder and killing, it is perhaps refreshing to read how some British people kept their sense of proportion and tried not to be overcome by the events. In Robert's papers I found part of a personal diary entitled *Diary and Letters of Arthur Moffatt Lang, 1st Lieutenant Bengal Engineers - India 1857 to 1859*. Clearly the writer was a great admirer of Sir Robert, and this would explain how the latter came to possess a copy of the diary entries covering events at Lahore from January to May 1857. Lang was seconded to the Public Works Department as Executive Engineer, Lahore. British people in Northern India saw their world crash round them on 10th May 1857, including their very full social life, and the extracts below (not published till now) show how Lang viewed it all.[19]

2nd Jan. 1857 Friday Mian Mir
Up before gun-fire. Banes, Elliot Brownlow and I drove in my cart to Shalimar where our horses were waiting us. We ran and killed (jackal) very soon. Ran again but spent half an hour outside a sugar-cane field out of which, at last, came a huge wild cat! Later went to 49th NI for a grand champagne tiffin: a regular orgy it was.

3rd Jan.
Up late. Gymnastics. At 12 to a very nice champagne breakfast at Piercy's, about a dozen there. Afterwards EB, Walter and I drove down to Lahore, left the cart, and strolled round watching passers by haggling at shop fronts (imagining Arabian Nights). At sunset drove home and dined at the Artillery Mess.

On 14th April Lang went to a ball given by the 81st Foot, in Cantonments. He wrote about it the next day.

15th April Wednesday
It was a warm enough night for the ball tho' remarkably cool for this time of year. No punkahs but dancing was kept up as in the cold weather. Sir John Lawrence came for about ½-hour and looked very miserable. He suffers from pains in his face and altogether is overworked.

Lang attended the disarming parade at Mian Mir on 13th May and began his diary for that day with:

Gulliver (PWD) came in before dawn. Up I jumped and we rode off to the Grand Parade to join the Brigadier's staff. Mr Montgomery, Roberts, Egerton, Deputy Commissioner, etc. were there.

Later Lang commented about the parade:

The sepoys are very much cut up about it and declare they would, on their own parades, have obeyed orders and given up their arms: but they are very much hurt at the loaded guns and the European artillery. We must be thankful that no *émeute* took place this morning. Mrs Boileau, her daughters, and Mrs Rumley were there in a carriage, very anxious to see the result. I slept nearly all day. At the Band as usual in the evening.

On 14th May Lang wrote:

The inhabitants of Lahore City are in such a jolly panic: my baboos have been imploring to be let off early, as they didn't eat anything this morning, in terror of the sepoys rising. I don't know how it is that I can't feel the danger as it ought to be felt. I'm either apathetic or stupid, and I feel occasionally the *pleasure* of the excitement. I pity the poor ladies, their fears for their kith and kin.

16th May Saturday
Another day gone, and we are all going on comfortably. I dined last night at the Montgomerys and all his party came, all Anarkullieites, Mrs Richard Lawrence and the Ommaney ladies (Chief Engineer's family). All ladies live in the Fort or the European barracks. The civilian men sleep in a tent by Mr Montgomery's. We had a pleasant enough evening, music, etc. Twenty rupees a head offered for all deserters brought in. We are to have no regular service tomorrow, but Farrer (chaplain) is going to the Artillery barracks and to 81st.

18th May Monday
I visited Lahore Fort today, and heard such stories of the flight to get there. Ladies came 8 or 9 in a carriage and ran into the Gateways, their children in their arms, at 2 o'clock on a May day! I slept, as I always do, like a top, and at about two was shaken out of my senses nearly by my bearer. 'Stand to your arms.' I felt very inclined to go on sleeping, and was disgusted to hear, as I came grumbling up, buckling on my sword, that it was a false alarm again. I

believe we are to have the ladies from Sialkot in here, and a European regiment is coming by river steamer from Karachi to join us.

Later on Lieutenant Lang was transferred to the Delhi Field, where he played an active and very gallant part in the final stage of the assault on the city. About this the History of the Royal Bengal Engineers says:

> On the night of September 13th two engineer officers, Lieutenants Lang and Medley, crept down into the ditch, examined the condition of the breaches in the walls, and, though fired upon by the enemy, they succeeded in getting back unhurt, and reported the breaches practicable for the assault.

The final attack, leading to the capture of the city, began the next day. Lang lived on until 1916, when he died at Guildford, aged 83. He had lived to see World War I, with sappers of his Bengal Engineers sent to France to fight for their King Emperor against alien white men.

During August 1857, after John Nicholson had arrived at the Delhi Ridge, my grandfather evidently made a serious mistake in his judgement of a senior army officer. By now the Grand Trunk Road had nearly reached the Sutlej and was metalled as far as Ferozepore, just south of the river. Ferozepore was therefore all-important, not only as roadhead but as the strategic base from which to maintain and protect the precarious communications with Delhi, 250 miles to the south east. Lt. Elphinstone's letter, quoted earlier, shows how very disturbed all Cis-Sutlej territory was.

The commander at Ferozepore was General Van Cortlandt, CB, who had a distinguished military career earned during his exploits in both Sikh Wars, and before that when he served with the Sikh army of Ranjit Singh. After the Mutiny began he was seconded to the Punjab Government, and Sir John Lawrence sent him to Ferozepore with orders to raise locally the Haryana Field Force for the tasks indicated above. This force was really a private army of Van Cortlandt, who commanded it admirably and was most successful in all he did. From Ferozepore he sent twenty dispatches, between 25th June and 26th August, to Lahore, reporting his actions, all of which Robert kept and acknowledged. No record or history of the Mutiny period criticises Van Cortlandt, yet suddenly Robert sends the following personal letter to Sir John, written in manuscript ink, undated and with no address.

1857

My dear John,
    I send 2 sets of dispatches from Van Cortlandt. You will see that 300 of the Bikanir troops as also a Tehsildar and Thanahdar of ours have been cut up.
    I think Cortlandt greatly wanting in energy. Had he pitched into the Jumalpore men 15 days ago they would have been broken and dispersed, and

they would have no pluck for anything. As it is they now present a formidable front and all the disaffected gather round them. The 10th Cavalry sowars (some of them) have joined them. Cortlandt will have to fight a regular battle and if he does not look out the whole population will rise.

Yours afftly
R. Montgomery

Sir John Lawrence, KCB

I have seen no evidence that Robert's fears were justified; however he managed to get back the original manuscript of the above letter and he kept it!

In 1857 Delhi was a city of splendour and brilliance with stately mosques and minarets, walled gardens bright with beautiful flowers, lovely fountains of white marble, crowded bazaars and streets offering luxuries of every kind; of course there were attractive dancing girls, snake charmers and other animal tamers, jugglers, fortune tellers and the like, all with high reputations and gathered from every part of Asia, not just India. The city was also renowned as a centre of a traditional Muslim culture, developed under the Mughal Emperors who encouraged painters and theologians, musicians and poets, architects and builders, to come to their capital. Yet within this wondrous city, surrounded by walls of red sandstone more than twenty feet high and entered by eleven gates, there were signs of dirt and decay; for the military and political power of the Mughal dynasty had ended. Only the King's Palace (the Red Fort as we called it, built by Shah Jehan and now well known to countless thousands of tourists) remained, as the symbol of the last of the Mughal Emperors whom the British had not yet formally deposed.

This was the setting for the famous siege of Delhi which began early on the morning of Monday 11th May, when sowars of the 3rd Cavalry, from the mutineers at Meerut, crossed the Bridges of Boats, under the very walls of the King's Palace, and cantered up to the Calcutta Gate; they found it open, entered the city, and rode for the Palace. This moment in time heralded the start of the real mutiny, for if all the city gates had been kept shut the rebels could not have entered and much precious time would have been gained; time to warn the authorities and to *act*. As it was the city was taken entirely by surprise that morning, and the stage was set inevitably for the long mutiny that followed. Had there been one British regiment in the Delhi Garrison the situation might yet have been saved, in spite of the outbreak at Meerut on the evening of the 9th. A brief description follows of that first morning in Delhi, as Indians saw it.[20]

All Muslims were up early to eat before the sun rose, as the month of the Ramadan Fast was not yet over, whilst Hindus were bathing early in the Jumna as usual. The British Resident and Commissioner, Mr Simon Fraser, was still in bed at his modern home, Ludlow Castle, not far outside the Kashmir Gate, and the Collector, Mr Hutchinson, was about to go to the Court House; no one knew of the events at Meerut, and it was a dreadfully hot morning. The papers had arrived from Calcutta the previous day and there had been no hint of trouble. Professor Ramchandra had risen early to go to Delhi College, on the bank of the Jumna, where the Faculties always met early in the summer, and Mainuddin Hassan, officer in charge of Paharganj Police Station was already in court waiting for the Collector. Munshi Jivanlal was on his way to court; he was clerk to Captain Douglas, the British officer commanding the Palace Guards.

That summer morning had begun so normally and so peacefully but suddenly it all changed. When the sowars arrived at the Palace they saw an Indian Christian, Dr Chamanlal, standing in front of his Dispensary, and immediately killed him with their sabres; he was the first casualty inside the city. The sowars then invited the Palace Guard to join them, which they did, and they all went together to the royal apartments calling on the King to assume command and lead them, as their Emperor, in their fight for their religion. In situations such as this news travels like the wind, and when Simon Fraser and Mr Hutchinson rushed to the Palace to join Captain Douglas they were all three killed at once. The 38th Native Infantry, on duty in the city, joined the mutineers and so did all troops in the Cantonment on the Ridge. That finally settled the fate of Delhi.

What followed is a matter of history, already so often told; including the fierce battles and high casualties, the looting and destruction, until the final attack on the city on 14th September, headed by John Nicholson who was mortally wounded as, sword in hand, he led the last bloody assault on the Kashmir Gate.

At this stage in my story it is well to recall how the horrors of the Indian Mutiny tend to obscure the many remarkable deeds of British gallantry, courage and heroism that occurred during the campaign, and should be equally well known. In all 182 VCs were won by British officers and men during the Mutiny, being exactly the same number as were to be awarded in the whole six years of the World War II. The first five of the Mutiny Victoria Crosses were won on that Monday 11th May, by officers and their British Assistants of the Bengal Artillery who defended, and finally blew up, the vast Delhi magazine lest it fall into rebel hands; the eldest of these five heroes was sixty-five, and the oldest man ever to be awarded the VC[21]. I believe that deeds such as these fostered those high traditions of loyalty and self-sacrifice that lived on within all ranks of the Indian Army into our day, and are still there in the new armies of the subcontinent.

In Sir Robert's records I came across the reports of secret agents, sent into Delhi to obtain intelligence of the rebel army's strength and dispositions, their state of morale and intentions, with, above all, the degree of the King's influence, or lack of it, on the mutineers. I found forty-one such reports, produced by nineteen separate agents, covering the period from 2nd June until the final surrender of the city on 16th September. Each report begins with the identity of the agent, shown by his name (true or false we do not know) and the date of the report; sometimes 'spy' is added after the name (e.g. 'Man Singh, Spy'), but there is no other reference to identity, except in one case where the source is described as 'Captain Hodson's Munshi'; the names are invariably Muslim or Hindu. Evidently this whole network was organised and controlled by Hodson, who was responsible to the civil authorities only, for the original Urdu script of each report was always delivered in the first place to George Barnes, Commissioner for the Cis-Sutlej states at Ambala. Hodson's name never appears except in the one case referred to above.

Barnes had each report translated, generally by his Assistant Commissioner, George Lewin, and he then personally signed each English language version before forwarding it to the Chief Commissioner at Lahore. For security reasons this material was never referred to openly except by its cover title 'The Delhi News', and each report was headed 'Delhi News' without any security classification. We do not know how many copies of the English language translations, if any, were made; all that is certain is that Robert, at Lahore, received these reports and retained them personally, and that John Lawrence's initials appear on most of them. We can only hope that the Army Commander on the Ridge also saw the material, or some accurate version of it, particularly the order of battle intelligence to which I refer below. An example of the 'Delhi News' is included in the Appendix to this book; Robert also possessed some of the original Urdu manuscripts. Altogether he kept ten of these vernacular scripts, which leads me to suppose that they, and the forty-one English translations, are very rare, and possibly unique of their kind. For these are the reports of secret agents who were infiltrated into Delhi *during* the seige and reported back to the British *at the time*, not after victory had been won; in this important sense they differ from published reports about siege conditions in the city which were written long after the Mutiny was over.

THE DELHI NEWS
(some brief paraphrased extracts)

July 14th. Barnes forwards a long and very comprehensive order of battle of the Rebel Army, showing separately the strength and locations of cavalry, artillery and infantry regiments, both inside and outside the city, as deployed in depth to defend the Palace, and every Gate and Bastion on the walls; the exact positions of forty 24-pounder (heavy) artillery pieces and 30 light artillery field guns are shown. Total rebel strength amounts to 5,500 cavalry, 15,000 infantry and 6,500 Ghazis and fanatics, excluding all artillerymen. A comprehensive report, or synopsis of it, was probably concealed between the inner and outer sole of a shoe, or in a coat lining, or in the mouth, in order to smuggle it out. To memorise so much precise detail would be impossible.

July 19th. Ranji Dass reports that cow killing in the city had begun. But the King has ordered that anyone guilty of killing a cow shall be blown away from guns. However the sepoys rule in Delhi, not the old King. 50,000 mutineers now in the city. The translation of this report is shown in the Appendix.

August 14th. Hurgobiad, spy. Reports very large numbers of Ghazis entering the city, ready to fight. The King is enriching his own family, and is demanding that the people pay him 10 lacs of rupees.

August 23rd. Merda Hurkara, spy. Reports how he entered the city but was arrested. He describes his adventures and how he got away out of the city.

September 6th. Gouri Shankar, spy. Reports the rebels know the siege train has arrived at the Ridge. The princes have left the city. The King says he is ready to die. Desertions are increasing.

It is well known that after Delhi had fallen the eventual fate of the rebel cause was doomed; though Lucknow was not relieved for many months. Bitter fighting, with very heavy casualties on both sides, continued until the end of 1857, and the Mutiny was not completely suppressed until April 1859. My grandfather became much involved in these later stages of the rebellion after he was appointed Chief Commissioner of Oudh, and I have dealt separately with this controversial period of his life in the chapter that follows. Looking again though at the siege of Delhi and its significance in the final outcome of the conflict, it is worthwhile recording what Indians today regard as the root cause for the collapse of the rebellion. The Hindu writer Savarkar was quite certain that this lay in the Punjab when he wrote:

> Although the revolutionary party tried their utmost, the Sikhs of the Punjab turned to the side of the English. In short on account of the treachery of the Sikhs and the premature rising at Meerut, the roots of the revolution were all weeded out. And the Punjab being the back-bone of Delhi, the news was very discouraging to the patriots.

How pleased Thomason would have been by such words! He had sent all his best men to the Punjab, and it was Dr Sen who wrote: 'The administration (of the province) was run by a band of very able men, in fact the pick of the civil service had been drafted to the Punjab from the older provinces.'

7
Oudh

At home in Ireland my uncle James Montgomery wrote the following:

Early in 1858, soon after the final relief of Lucknow, my father Sir Robert Montgomery left Lahore and went to Oudh as Chief Commissioner; meanwhile, a month or so later, mother took us all to Missouri for the hot weather, as being nearer to Lucknow than Dharmsala. I was then eight years old and was sent as a day-boy to Dr Maddox's school, riding each way on my pony. Charlie Muir, son of Sir William Muir the well-known writer and Indian administrator, was a frequent companion on my daily rides. That autumn we went down to Lucknow for the first time and I well remember the house, Bank's Bungalow, on the South Eastern outskirts of the city, which my father then had as his residence. The place was misnamed a bungalow, for it was a grand and imposing building with an upper storey for all the bedrooms, and stood in a big compound with a large garden surrounded by high walls.

The house had evidently been attacked for, with several buildings in the compound, it bore many marks of bullets and other missiles. At the gate there was a guard room for native soldiers, who always turned out to salute the Chief Commissioner whenever he left the house and returned.

The guard mounting fascinated me and I was determined to have my own guard. I got some old muskets and tulwars and drilled my younger brother Ferguson, and the chuprassis; one day, when my father drove up to the house in his carriage, he was very amused to see me commanding a small squad, and heard a shrill voice call out: 'Guard, Present Arms'!

The schoolmaster of the 88th Foot (Connaught Rangers) used to come and give us lessons, until the first week in January 1859 when Ferguson and I were sent home to school. Father and mother drove with us the forty miles from Lucknow to Cawnpore, where we were put in charge of Mr and Mrs Smaile who took us on to Benares, partly by river and partly by road. This road journey was very slow for we travelled in dak-garis, drawn, not by horses but by men! I suppose all the horses at every stage had been either commandeered or stolen; the men drew the garis at a walk and were relieved at villages (or pressed into service) on our route. One day some Indian mounted police told us to stop because armed mutineers (both sowars and sepoys) were approaching not far off. On hearing this our 'human horses' all bolted at once, and left us stranded! Fortunately we were not attacked and with fresh relays of coolies we eventually reached Benares. At Benares the Rev. Leupoldt, a CMS missionary, and his wife took us on to Calcutta and from there by sea to England. A faithful old muslim servant, Hussaini (he was always our friend and standby) accompanied us all the way from Lucknow to London, as he had done when my brother Henry (Bishop Montgomery) went home a few years earlier, before the Mutiny began.

James Alexander Lawrence Montgomery, my grandfather's third son, wrote the above account in 1869, after leaving Harrow and before joining his regiment, the 92nd (later Gordon) Highlanders. Sir Robert had purchased a commission for James, as an Ensign in infantry (it cost £250 in those days!). He must have been one of the last generation of British officers to purchase their commission; the system was dropped a few years later. Uncle Jimmie, as we always called him, very soon transferred to the Indian Staff Corps - later the ICS. Thereafter he served many years in the Punjab and prospered exceedingly, becoming Commissioner of Rawalpindi Division; after which he was seconded as the Commissioner for Lands and Settlement in Kenya, until he finally retired in 1916. He always retained his Staff Corps (Indian military) promotion and pension rights, and so reached the rank of full Colonel in the Indian Army, having been awarded the CSI and CBE, after forty-seven years' service - though he was only a soldier for four years. He was rather proud of this, but he did not equal Sir Robert's record of being a commissioned officer in the Bengal Engineers without even one day's service in the army!

Lord Canning, the Governor-General, had telegraphed to my grandfather on 21st March, the very day that Lucknow was finally relieved, requesting him to take over the Commissionership of Oudh from Sir James Outram, as soon as possible. That day was the first of two dates, both of far-reaching significance for the history of British rule in all India, and particularly for the ruler of Oudh province. Canning issued his famous confiscation decree on 21st March, in which he proclaimed, in the name of the East India Company, that proprietary rights in the soil of Oudh were to be confiscated by the Government of India, with the exception of six specially exempted estates - the owners of which had distinguished themselves by their support of the Company during the Mutiny. All remaining land in Oudh was to be confiscated, 'and disposed of in such manner as the Government of India might consider expedient'. Coming so soon after the deposition of Wajid Ali Shah, the last Muslim King of Oudh, with the annexation of his country, this proclamation at once raised a great storm, reviving and indeed increasing the controversy over land rights and tenure that had so bedevilled the Sleeman and Thomason era.

The second significant date was 1st November 1858 when Lord Canning, on behalf of Queen Victoria, proclaimed that the long rule of the Honourable East India Company was over. The British crown would rule all India as the paramount power, both in the Provinces and in the States, where all treaties and engagements made with Native Princes by the East India Company would remain inviolate, and be scrupulously maintained . . . so ran the proclamation. 'The Company's' rule lasted so long (it had become traditional) that its abolition would create enormous problems, political, military, social, administrative and economic. Lord Canning himself made this proclamation at a great ceremony at Allahabad. Wearing his court dress, standing under a canopy of crimson and gold, accompanied by civil and military officers in their dress uniforms, and surrounded by nobles and princes wearing scarlet, the first Viceroy (for such Canning now became) read out the proclamation in English; it was then read again in Urdu and a salute of twenty-one guns followed. 'The Company' that Robert had served for thirty years had gone and, with hundreds of other British officers, he was now a member of the Indian Civil Service directly under the Queen, though not yet the Queen Empress. My grandfather should have attended that ceremony at Allahabad, but, as will be seen, problems pressed upon him and he could not leave Lucknow.

Robert was no stranger to Lucknow, he had often been there while he was at Cawnpore and he knew the climate of the Ganges Valley well; so he was not surprised to find the temperature was reaching 108°F in the shade when he arrived at Bank's Bungalow in the first week of April. But his whole lifestyle was to change, for he was now, in name and fact, the head and ruler of a province; similar in rights and privilege to the position of a provincial Lieutenant-Governor. When he arrived on 3rd April he was received for the first time with a salute of fifteen guns. More important to him was his salary, which was increased to 5500 rupees a month, though that was still not sufficient for all his needs.

My grandfather had no part in the famous siege of Lucknow which lasted for nearly ten months with so much loss of human life; its first personal impact had been the death of his oldest friend Sir Henry Lawrence, in the Residency on 4th July. Major Banks - of Bank's Bungalow - had succeeded Sir Henry as Chief Commissioner, but he too had been killed on 21st July (shot through the head during an assault on the Western face of the Residency defences), and it was Banks' house in which Robert now lived. Above all else however was the plain fact that the recapture of Lucknow was not a military victory in the sense that all hostilities were ended. The Grand Trunk Road was safe and communications had once more been opened between Bengal and the Punjab, Calcutta and Lahore. But rebel armies had dispersed into Oudh and

Rohilkhand, whilst, very unfortunately, the Begum of Oudh, Hazrat Mahal, a mistress of the ex-King and a prominent leader of the rebels in Lucknow, had got away with her son. Later on, Robert was to have dealings with her.

Robert's staff at Lucknow included some members who had been right through the siege and had survived to continue under his administration. They told him of the awful ravages of cholera, dysentery, and malnutrition, as well as the immense privations and hardship, particularly lack of food, that the besieged garrison had suffered. Improvisation had been uppermost in everyone's mind, and one British family finally produced sparrow curry for their dinner, made from 150 sparrows slaughtered for the meal; it was pronounced delicious! In the military sense the most desperate period was possibly the eight weeks at the Residency between Havelock and Outram's reinforcement of the garrison late in September 1857, and Sir Colin Campbell's second relief of the city on 17th November. It was during this period that Thomas Henry Kavanagh, a British civilian clerk in the Deputy Commissioner's office, had won the Victoria Cross. Kavanagh was still working in that office when Robert arrived and he stayed on there as an Assistant Commissioner. The story of Kavanagh's exploits fascinated my grandfather, who took care to keep an eight-page manuscript letter that Kavanagh sent to him at Bank's Bungalow.

When the relief force was approaching Lucknow on 13th November, Outram knew it was essential that Campbell should have the services of a British guide, familiar with the city, in order to avoid its tortuous streets, before the actual advance on the Residency. Kavanagh volunteered to slip through the rebel lines in and beyond the city, which were very strongly held, and convey Outram's plans and information to Sir Colin Campbell. A Hindu scout, Kananj Lal, would go with Kavanagh but the latter was six feet tall with piercing blue eyes and, whatever his disguise, Kananj Lal feared that his accent would inevitably betray them both if they were intercepted. Eventually Kavanagh persuaded Kananj Lal to accompany him and Outram agreed; Kavanagh then painted his face and body entirely with lamp black and wore a dirty yellow silk *kurta* (long-skirted coat) with a pink turban, tight muslim trousers and country-made shoes; he looked completely the part he had chosen, as a Lucknow *badmash* or robber, and Outram himself failed to recognise him. The latter concealed the letter from Outram to Campbell in the folds of his paggri cloth.

The couple passed through the British lines at night without difficulty and moved to the Gumti River, which they followed upstream, and then waded across to the left bank to approach the city as if they had come down from the north. They recrossed the Gumti by the old stone bridge and entered the city, where they found the streets neither crowded nor well lighted, and safely reached open country to the south. There they lost

their way till they met two women who helped them find the right track –
to the Cawnpore road. Next they blundered straight into a rebel picquet
and were seized, tied up, and questioned by the sepoys. But Kananj Lal
contrived to do all the talking, whilst Kavanagh wept and wailed, and they
were allowed to go on. However they soon fell into a swamp and had to
wade knee-deep through muddy water for two hours. By this time
Kavanagh was utterly exhausted, and, worse still, the lamp black had
almost vanished from his hands, the moon was waning and dawn could
not be far off! They did not know where the British camp was, or indeed
their own position, and Kavanagh felt he could not go any further and
must sleep in a mango grove where they had halted; this he promptly did
and sent Kananj Lal away to find a village and ask for a guide. Then,
suddenly, luck intervened and they were challenged by a Sikh horseman
from an Indian cavalry patrol of Campbell's army; unwittingly they had
finished up in the right area and were taken to the British headquarters
and the Commander-in-Chief's tent. Kavanagh wrote: 'As I approached
the tent an elderly gentleman with a stern face came out, and going up to
him I asked for Sir Colin Campbell. "I am Sir Colin Campbell", the old
man said [he was 65], and I took off my turban and gave him Sir James
Outram's letter.'

In addition to the Victoria Cross, which a civilian can win when under
military command, Kavanagh was rewarded by a grant of 20,000 rupees,
with his promotion to Assistant Commissioner. Kananj Lal got 5,000
rupees and was appointed Tehsildar, with villages assessed at 837 rupees
per annum *settled* on him.

At this stage I believe it essential to outline the physical setting of
Lucknow, at the time when Robert arrived there, and describe his
reactions to what he found. The Residency and the buildings nearby,
including the English church, were all in ruins, and extensive damage had
been done to the vast fortress of Machchi Bhavan facing the Gumti River.
Many palaces and mosques, famous for their religious character and
significance, and their beauty of design and style, had suffered terribly in
all the fighting and artillery bombardment. The Great Imambara, the
architectural gem of Lucknow, built in the eighteenth century by the
Nawab Asf-o-dowla, showed great gaps in its walls. The building known as
the Little Imambara, the tomb of the 4th King of Oudh, was equally
damaged; as also was the Hoseinabad Imambara, said to rival any other
building in the city in beauty of detail. But the Kaiser Bagh, renowned as
the site of corruption and debauchery practised by the Oudh kings, had
not suffered so much. The Nawab Wajid Ali Shah, deposed by the British
two years earlier, had completed the final stage of this huge edifice, but he
then gave himself up so thoroughly to enjoying it that he never did
anything else!

Probably the greatest destruction of all was at the Begum Kothi, where all the looting and wanton pillage of fabulous treasures took place, and with which Robert became involved when the Prize Agents began their assessment for the Government at Westminster. Of this incident, albeit equalled in its ferocity when rebel armies destroyed British property, Dr Sen wrote:

> The soldiers had broken into the store-rooms and pitched their contents into the court ... embroidered cloths, paintings, silver, gorgeous silk standards, diamonds, rubies, sapphires, emeralds, tiaras studded with jewels ... It was suspected by the troops that some small caskets, in battered cases, sufficient to redeem mortgages on certain large estates in Scotland, England and Ireland found their way inside officer's uniform cases! ... The Prize Agents estimated their total taking at a million and a quarter sterling.

Clearly Robert at once began to rebuild what had been destroyed, and his choice of function for new construction, and the priorities he ordered, reveal so well his character and attitude to the events of his time. Here is a draft memorandum in his own handwriting, written in April, addressed to his secretary, Douglas Forsyth.

Memo

April 1858

The rebels have utterly destroyed our beautiful Residency church. In like manner the church in Cantonments has been shamefully desecrated; nothing has been left but the bare walls, and the mural tablets have been smashed.

I consider that the first new building to be erected in Lucknow should be a church, and it will be paid for out of the money raised by the fine which I have directed to be levied on the city. It is only fair that the inhabitants should pay for the rebuilding of our holy temples which they have destroyed. Two churches will be required, and nothing need hinder one being built immediately at the Civil Station, which will be available also for the troops until their new Cantonment church is erected.

Write to the General and say that I shall feel obliged by his issuing orders to all officers in command of troops to preserve the public buildings they occupy from being injured or defaced – that already extensive injury has been done to numerous buildings and statues and vases have been broken or carried away. Arrange for gardens and men to look after them.

R. M.

As a result of these instructions the Kaiser Bagh was allotted to the Church Missionary Society, which announced: 'The building which witnessed so much debauchery will now be the source of spiritual welfare, whence light and life will spring on Muslim and Pagan of Lucknow.' The Little Imambara was given to the Church of Scotland and the Great

Imambara handed over as barracks for British infantry. The new church for the civil station was sited close to the walls of the park enclosing Bank's Bungalow - how wise of Robert! An article in *The Times* (16th October 1858) about restoration in Lucknow included the following:

> The great hall of audience (of the Kaiser Bagh), which no European was ever allowed to enter, is now crowded by 500 soldiers to witness theatrical entertainments ... In short Mr Montgomery is using his absolute power wisely, and in another year will have turned this Indian Sodom into the most European of Asiatic cities. Lucknow now has a regular patrolling police, on the London model, with a native *Christian* inspector to each division. Strict rules have been introduced for cleanliness, and 'necessaries' - things totally unknown in India where the people are still primitive - have been planted all over the city, and fines are inflicted for any refusal to use them.

Looking back, was Robert Montgomery right in his use, or misuse, of sacred Muslim sites? No government funds were allotted for new construction of mosques or other non-Christian buildings. However my grandfather certainly appears as a reformist before his time with his 'necessaries' in Lucknow city. In no other Indian cities, at that time, were there properly constructed public drainage systems or any form of street lavatories; drinking water for Indian nationals was still carried in goat skins filled from ponds in which everybody bathed, though the ponds were usually covered with slime!

Maybe it was these 'necessaries', that Robert introduced, which played a part in keeping him and Ellen so free from the customary health hazards during the remainder of their Indian service! Meanwhile Ellen much enjoyed Lucknow after her return from Missouri. She was now the wife of the Chief Commissioner with all the prestige that went with it, besides her obligations for work and interest in charity organisations, welfare and church committees, that flourished in her time, as in our day. But she had leisure for riding, or driving, in Dilkhusa Park close to Bank's Bungalow - it seems always to have been called that and not the Residency. She also liked the open country that became the Horticultural Gardens, further east along the right bank of the Gumti. Dilkhusa Palace had been a hunting box and country residence of the Oudh kings, much favoured by the ladies of the Harem, and not far from the Shah Munzil where the celebrated wild beast fights had taken place. The smaller animals were put to fight inside the enclosure of the Shah Munzil, including combats between tigers and panthers, and always with strong animal cages and safe arenas for the audience. But fights between exceptionally strong and heavy beasts, like elephants, rhinoceros, and buffaloes, were held on level ground on the opposite bank of the Gumti, where they could be viewed at a safe distance by the King and his ladies, from the verandahs of the Shah Munzil.

Strangely, these fights seem never to have been particularly exciting, as if the wild beasts had no stomach for them. The elephants were never defeated by any other beast, and a tiger could not win against a buffalo. These fights had been abandoned by the time Oudh was annexed but it was always interesting to view the scene of such historic events so popular with the royal family of Oudh.

My grandfather greatly regretted the disappearance of the Tarawalli Kothi, or Observatory, built by the first King of Oudh, adjoining the Horticultural Gardens. A British officer, Colonel Wilcox, had been Astronomer Royal and had advised on the purchase of the valuable scientific equipment. However the Colonel died in 1847 and Wajid Ali Shah - that profligate monarch - promptly closed down the establishment. All the astronomical instruments had been carefully stored away, but were never seen again. During the siege the Maulvi Ahmadullah Shah (known as the 'Danka' Shah because he always had a drum beaten before him wherever he went!) made the Observatory his headquarters, and his sepoys probably looted or destroyed everything. The Maulvi was a noted fighting soldier and the best leader the mutineers ever had.

In Oudh overall, Robert's main problems stemmed from the impact of the 1856 annexation of the province; after the Mutiny the population were left disaffected and angry, and distrustful of the Company's raj which so many thought had ended. It was a complicated situation made more so by the effect of Canning's confiscation decree. Volumes have been written on this whole subject, but my concern is with the eleven crucial months of Robert's Chief Commissionship at Lucknow. In those far distant days a Chief Commissioner, or Lieutenant-Governor, of a province had virtually absolute fiscal, legal and administrative power; the Governor-General at Calcutta issued his instructions and it was then the responsibility of the Chief Commissioner to implement them at his discretion. In practice he could make or mar the results, depending on his own opinions and orders, and his degree of leadership and control over his subordinate commissioners; the underlying factors were the great distances and the effects of climate and poor communications, which left him largely free to act without interference. In later years my grandfather told Bishop Montgomery how he had acted in these circumstances, in Oudh, with his own personal views on the Oudh problems and their background. The Bishop, fortunately, recorded the gist of these talks, which follows, supplemented by comments and criticisms of Robert's performance in works already published.

Lord Dalhousie had been Governor-General for eight years in 1856. He was a strong character, who genuinely loved the Indian peoples and was unsparing in his efforts in order, as he saw it, to bring justice and liberty to oppressed populations. He therefore travelled widely and, in pursuit of these aims, annexed much independent Indian state territory to British rule - Burma (Pegu), Sind, The Punjab and, finally, Oudh. In this light it is easy to see why Dalhousie strongly supported Thomason's settlement policy, in favour of the yeoman, or village, proprietors. In Oudh he aimed to end a land revenue system by which virtually all rent and land taxes went to swell the coffers of the Nawab, and his own immediate (feudal) subordinates, the Taluqdars. The best way to do this, in his view, was to impose on all classes the *settlement* which had clearly been so successful under Thomason and in the Punjab.

It was a tragedy, Robert said, that the Mutiny came just at the change of Governors-General. Dalhousie had twice toured the Punjab and had seen it all himself, but he did not have time before he left India in February 1856 to do the same for Oudh. Then Canning came and did not, perhaps could not, visit Oudh before the Mutiny, and the British civil administration officers in the province (inevitably pending its annexation) were a mere handful. Furthermore the British troops in Oudh were reduced, by Canning, to one weak infantry regiment and one battery of artillery. How different results might have been if there had been no such reduction?

So Dalhousie's settlement plans for Oudh after its annexation were not fully carried out. Outram, the Resident at Lucknow, became the first Chief Commissioner, but almost at once had to go on furlough. His place was taken by Coverley Jackson, who was by no means so fitted for a very difficult situation, and trouble quickly followed. Of Coverley Jackson, Dr Sen wrote:

> If Sir James Outram had continued as Chief Commissioner, probably adequate measures would have been adopted in time to reconcile the people, adversely affected, to the new order ... Jackson lacked the sympathetic imagination that his new office demanded. He appropriated for his own residence a palace reserved for the members of the Oudh royal family. He was subsequently censured for his indiscretion and had to quit the palace, but public feeling had already been outraged ...

A year later, in March 1857, Coverley Jackson was removed and Henry Lawrence took the office. 'See what damage a Chief Commissioner left alone for 12 Months can do,' Robert said. For by then it was too late and the Mutiny broke out two months afterwards. In effect then, the 1856 annexation of Oudh was, in part, a *non-sequitur*, in terms of actual change for the majority of the rural (peasant) population before the Mutiny began; this seems to bear out the quotation by Dr Pragdish Raj on page 52 of this book.

It is a matter of history how the worst then occurred - at least for the protagonists of Oudh annexation. For the village proprietors, whose rights and liberties were supposed to have been restored by the annexation act, joined in the Mutiny on the side of the taluqdars from whose thralls the act was designed to save them! Dr Pragdish Raj wrote of this development:

> The villagers acted, in fact, as though they regarded the arrangements made at the (annexation) settlement as valid, and to be maintained, *just so long as British rule lasted* [my italics]. Montgomery likewise argued, from the events of the Mutiny, that they had tended to show that entire release from a condition of subordination to the taluqdars was not universally desired by the village proprietors.

Dr Sen supported Montgomery in this view when he wrote 'The Mutiny, in Oudh, proved that the native rule was not so unpopular after all . . . It was the belief that the British cause was hopeless that led the taluqdars openly to rebel.'

In these quotations we see again, in the minds of sepoys of the Bengal army and of so many Indian nationals, that the British raj had ended; equally, prophets had said the Company's rule would end 100 years after the battle of Plassey in 1757. We have already seen how it did end on 1st November 1858. But does this mean that without Dalhousie's annexation act there might have been no mutiny in Oudh? Some writers say 'yes' whilst retaining the word 'might'; but surely looking again at the province as a whole, with eleven million people, it is illogical to visualise how Oudh could have remained a vacuum, immune from the events of 1857-58. What is certain is that a definite vacuum, full of great potential trouble, did appear directly Lord Canning issued his drastic decree - 'All proprietary rights in the soil (of Oudh) were to be confiscated by the Government of India . . .' My grandfather arrived at Bank's Bungalow within a week of this proclamation's issue; it meant, in effect, that, with few exceptions, the landed aristocracy of Oudh would lose all their ancestral property, and that they, and all village proprietors as well, must make immediate submission to the Chief Commissioner by surrendering their arms and obeying his orders. We see next how Robert Montgomery dealt with this sudden crisis.

My grandfather's solution to this very difficult problem has been briefly, but very accurately, described by Dr Pragdish Raj who wrote, in *The Mutiny and British Land Policy*:

> . . . In the absence of any written evidence, it is perhaps impossible to know Canning's real intentions in issuing the proclamation. It is feasible that it was originally intended to punish the taluqdars but later on was twisted to another end. For this change Outram[22] and Montgomery appear responsible. Sir James Outram protested against the proclamation. Sir Robert Montgomery quietly locked it away in his desk, and sent out an invitation to all the chiefs to surrender, couched in the very opposite terms. Outram and Montgomery justified their actions on grounds of military and political expediency. Their

view is difficult to understand ... The taluqdars were surely not so powerful as to deserve such lavish conciliation.

To put it another way, Robert appreciated that the proclamation was wrong in principle and would be bad in practice. He therefore decided to ignore it! He then proceeded quietly but firmly with his own brand of solution; this, briefly, was to 'follow the middle way', as he had done so successfully at Lahore when at the centre of the John and Henry Lawrence fracas. In this instance he would contact and 'treat' (conciliate if you like but not confiscate!) with the taluqdars, whilst preserving and improving all existing rights and liberties of village proprietors. Meanwhile he would concentrate on the realities of the problems in his province, which, as he saw it, meant action on the following lines - I have tabulated these six 'needs' as he called them:

1. Try to put fire in the military authorities - we shall see why he thought this necessary!
2. Reorganise the police - a vital task.
3. Disarm the population.
4. Enact a new civil code of law.
5. Woo the taluqdars.
6. Settle the land revenue and ownership rights.

Evidently Robert was successful in solving the last two requirements, the outcome of which would largely depend on the action taken on the other four. The *Oxford History of India* (Vincent Smith) has this to say of the Oudh pacification immediately following the mutiny:

> The application of the principles of general confiscation, and re-grants (of land) to suitable persons, were wisely left to the discretion of Mr Montgomery, the Chief Commissioner of Oudh. The province was settled on terms sufficiently satisfactory to the great landlords, with adequate arrangements for the protection of under proprietors and tenants ...'

Sometimes, when issuing 're-grants to suitable persons', Robert encountered a peculiarly oriental outlook; an Oudh taluqdar would think it incomprehensible that an Englishman should consider conferring land on an enemy whom he had defeated in battle.

In pursuing his 'middle way' policy my grandfather took the unusual step of writing personally to the Begum Hazrat Mahal; she was sometimes, though quite wrongly, called the Queen of Oudh and had always strongly opposed the annexation. After escaping from Lucknow she was planning fresh operations against the Raj, and to detach her from the rebel cause would help immensely in pacifying the province. Robert's letter, couched in polite terms and according her all the high-sounding royal titles she demanded, suggested her capitulation, in which case she would enjoy certain benefits and advantages, etc. ... The Begum's reply, written on rough rice paper in uneducated manuscript without any of the customary formalities, covered five foolscap pages in English translation, of which the following is a brief extract:

From the Begum to Mr Montgomery
Your eloquent letter of 23rd April 1858 has reached. In reply I beg to observe that whereas the Native Army mutinied for some reason or other, and came to Lucknow, I did not consider that I was doing any wrong in taking my seat on the throne of my ancestors – in conformity with ancient treaties which had been made with this family ... Your government took all my treasuries, my personal and real property, my houses ... and sold it by auction for money ... Although for a short time the villages were apparently relieved, yet all the Rajas, Taluqdars and nobility soon began to suffer ... It is quite contrary to our feelings to live without our religion and honour ... And let the English consider that never have the people [of Oudh] been so gratified and attached to any government as they are to MINE ...

Robert's attempt to win over the Begum was clearly a dismal failure! I have quoted from her letter because its uncompromising terms show so well the deep feelings against annexation among the nobility of Oudh, and also because I believe it may well be the only surviving[23], English language, version of her private correspondence. In the event her intransigence did not last and she was eventually won over; she accepted asylum, with her son and a small retinue, in Nepal, *and with a British pension*! But she never renounced her son's claim to be King of Oudh.

In April also, Lord Canning began his frequent correspondence with my grandfather, which, *inter alia*, heralded the latter's very strong criticism of the conduct of military operations in Oudh.

Allahabad

18th April 1858

Dear Mr Montgomery
A letter which I received yesterday from the C-in-C mentions one that has been addressed by Raja Man Singh to General Outram, as written in an improper tone, prescribing rather than seeking terms, and Sir Colin augurs ill from it. He is clearly apprehensive that resistance is becoming more organised and inveterate, instead of diminishing. Do you know anything of this letter from Man Singh? Pray send it to me if you have it ... It would be everything if we could secure to the side of government any one of the chiefs, of influence, and so give to the rest practical proof that they will be liberally treated.
The course which your letter describes as taken in settling the villages is exactly what I hoped to see done. Am I right in believing that you wish to

receive no instructions re the police until you have written on the subject?

I greatly fear that the recent check to the army at . . . [illegible] will lead to the C. in C.'s confining his operations within narrower bounds. If it has shaken his confidence in Gen. Walpole it will inevitably have this result.

Pray keep me fully informed of all symptoms of the disposition shown by the Chiefs.

Very faithfully yrs.
Canning

This letter shows clearly the *volte face* that Lord Canning made when he saw how very unpopular, and unwise, his confiscation decree had been; he now writes of 'liberal treatment' for the taluqdars. Raja Man Singh of Nawabganj always tried to be on good terms with both the rebels and the British, and generally professed allegiance to the Raj. We shall see later how Robert dealt with him! Meanwhile Canning became more and more appreciative of my grandfather's work.

Sir Colin Campbell had finally taken Lucknow with a force of 30,000 men and the rebel forces that remained, well led by Tantia Topi and the Rani of Jhansi (as well as the Begum of Oudh) were still fully armed and equipped and capable of hard fighting. But Robert Montgomery, mindful always of the need for quick decisions and speed in action, was convinced that if the army now showed energy and determination they should have little difficulty in defeating the rebels; mobile columns (memories of the Punjab!) were needed to harrass and pursue the enemy. During May he received a very long letter from Major-General Sir William Mansfield (Lord Clyde's Chief of Staff), about future military plans and intentions; a brief extract of this follows:

Camp Bareilly

14th May 1958

Dear Mr Montgomery

Immediately after receiving Barker's telegram of 10th announcing the rebel gathering at Nawabganj, orders were sent to General Grant to return to Lucknow with his Column, which will be quartered in the old Cantonment during the rains.

Until things are quieter than they are at present in Oudh it is absolutely necessary to keep all our available force at or about Lucknow. We have no troops to give you a Column, either towards Sitapore or Simdalla. We shall, I hope by Sept, have two or three battalions down from the Punjab, when it may be possible to replace General Walpole's Column by one of similar strength . . . In November we might reduce the strength here, but certainly not before that date.

We must have patience, and for the next few months content ourselves with what we have got – there is no help for it otherwise. It will then be seen,

101

viz after four or five months have elapsed, whether government will be able to launch an army into Oudh, with a dozen Columns at the same time . . . and subdue the country. At present we have not the numbers required for the reduction of your immense Province. Merely walking through it with two or three Columns without heavy guns is no good . . . I hope you will excuse me for venturing to intrude this on you.

I am yours very truly,
W. Mansfield

My grandfather was furious at receiving this letter, which he regarded as evidence of an intention, by the army, to remain in barracks, *doing nothing*, for five months until the cold weather came in November! He was accustomed to the ways of Nicholson, Lumsden, Hodson, etc., who struck at mutiny wherever they saw it, regardless of overwhelming (rebel) strength. In the Punjab the Frontier Force was under the Lahore government, but in Oudh the civil government had no control whatever over military matters; in Robert's view the army leaders in his province were not young, old-fashioned, reluctant to plan or take offensive operations, and altogether lacking in spirit.

Not surprisingly long and acrimonious correspondence followed! Robert kept it all but it is far too lengthy to include here. His chief accusation was a denunciation of the C-in-C in not attacking a force of 9000 rebels with 1200 British troops - 'we did it in the Punjab!' The army were incensed because they knew Robert's criticisms were also based on reports of the young civil serivce officers who accompanied each military column and reported direct to the Chief Commissioner. On 19th June the Chief of Staff sent a long dispatch to Lord Canning commenting very adversely on the acerbity of Robert's remarks about Campbell's alleged inactivity. Then the C-in-C himself wrote to Lord Canning: 'Montgomery does not understand the rules of war and need of caution; the roles of the civilian and the military differ.' However my grandfather would never actually apologise nor officially withdraw his words, though Ellen, when she heard about it at Missouri, was very apprehensive and feared the incident would damage her husband irretrievably!

It was not until the end of July that both men sent conciliatory letters to each other. Robert wrote first[24] and began: 'My dear Sir Colin', whereas Campbell replied: 'My dear Sir', but added: 'I am quite of your opinion that our public duty requires a complete cordiality between the Civil and Military officials - and I have no doubt that such a cordiality will always exist between you and myself.' What a change, for which Lord Canning was evidently responsible for he wrote to Robert on 20th July:

Dear Mr Montgomery
    I regret the controversial correspondence which has arisen between the

102

Military Authorities and yourself. Your Dispatch was taken up too angrily, and meanings were imputed to you of which you ought not to have been suspected. I will take care that you are set right in this respect. On the other hand I cannot absolve you of all share in what seems to be an almost universal error amongst Indian Service officers - expecting more from our Europeans [soldiers] than white flesh and blood can bear . . .'

Lord Canning obviously supported Robert, but would he have done so if he had not been so appreciative of the latter's work?

All that long hot summer my grandfather had to maintain a large household with all the ceremony and protocol inseparable from the office of Chief Commissioner. He did not really care for the social round, until later when Ellen had joined him, though he was invariably asked to attend functions of every kind; that dispute with the army did not help matters as the 'military' were always so much in evidence. The Lucknow garrison was very large, with regiments of cavalry, British and Indian infantry, and their supporting artillery and engineers. Robert therefore found it frustrating to read in the local newspaper: 'A reading room, library and coffee house near the Imambara will supply a want which Europeans in Lucknow will much enjoy. The energies of officers will be severely taxed to find amusements for their men during the summer and the rains, *when out of door exercise is impossible and there is no military occupation to engate them.*' (The italics are mine!)

A letter that Captain George Hutchinson, Robert's Military Secretary and a nephew by his first marriage, wrote to Samuel Montgomery at Moville mentions the pressure of work on the Chief Commissioner:

I find myself sitting in the next room to Uncle Robert actually holding the office of Military Secretary to him. It never entered my wildest dreams that he would come here and I should be so fortunate as to hold that office . . . Uncle R is very well and works as usual like two horses compressed into one; all day and every day, and at night if they can, he is besieged by visitors. We hope to have Ellen and the family here in the cold weather.

Everything in Oudh had to be refashioned with the police force almost the first priority, bearing in mind that a policeman was virtually armed and equipped as a soldier; there were 'police cavalry and police infantry', though not police artillery. My grandfather said this 'need' in Oudh could never have been satisfied without the help of Richard Lawrence, youngest of the five Lawrence brothers. Richard was now Commissioner of Police in the Punjab and readily responded to requests to send police contingents to Oudh. On 5th July he wrote to Robert from Murree:

Five magnificent squadrons of Mounted Police, and three Companies of Police Infantry, start from Lahore tomorrow for Lucknow - almost comes up to what you and I did in June and July 1857!

In the event Robert was able to raise a provincial police force of up to 12,000 horse and foot.

Robert and his Oudh administration well knew they could not claim the rebellion was ended so long as the bulk of the population, particularly the ex-sepoys, remained armed; men concerned in the murder of their officers still had to be apprehended and sentenced, and their offences written into the code of law. These were the main issues in which my grandfather personally intervened, trying to steer his 'middle way' between over-harshness and foolish leniency. His starting point was an astonishing proclamation by his predecessor Sir James Outram, decreeing that *every person* found in illegal possession of arms in Oudh after a certain date would be killed!

George Hutchinson left a manuscript note tabulating the Chief Commissioner's orders for the sentences, 'applicable to ex-sepoys of Regiments who had murdered their British officers':

All found guilty of such murder – Death
All concerned in such murder – Life may be spared

But this freedom from execution was on certain stringent conditions, one of which appears quite extraordinary: 'He must surrender his arms, but if he has no arms he must purchase some weapon and produce it instead'!

During January 1859 my grandfather, pursuing always his middle way, pardoned Raja Man Singh of Nawabganj who was always suspect (almost certainly true!) of assisting both the British and rebel armies. In return the Raja gave a grand ball at his palace outside Luknow. It was an amazing affair, reported at length in the London *Times* of 24th March 1859, of which an extract is below:

Lord Clyde was ill and could not attend, and Man Singh seemed to suspect his Lordship's illness was a *ruse*! The principal guests (General Mansfield and Mr Montgomery) rode to the ball on state elephants ... As the *Nautch* continued two Oudh girls of unusual ugliness, supported by eight men, kept up their endless swaying ... Then came eight boys dressed as girls, their faces covered with gold-leaf, who performed an abstruse comedy or mystery and sang a chorus of doubtful character (!) from which the company were diverted very pleasantly by an invitation to witness the fireworks, and then partake of supper ... The equipments of the table were imperfect – officers drank champagne out of soup plates and wine was spilt ... Had the night ended thus, all would have been well, but a captain of one of Her Majesty's regiments, who had not been invited to the ball, went up to Man Singh, snatched the Raja's gold embroidered cap from his head, and placed it on his own. To uncover the head of an Asiatic is a great insult, but one's host ... The uninvited captain (from the 23rd Foot[25]) slept there on a chair all night, and Man Singh is said to have made no complaint to General Sir William Mansfield ...

Unfortunately my grandfather left no comment on this party!

In those days the ambience of Lucknow was towards Islam; the city had been the capital of a historic royal kingdom and the mosques, palaces and forts were mainly Muslim in design and style. But the Oudh peasantry were of all classes, Hindu and Muslim, and in Robert's papers on Oudh he left a sheet of paper headed 'Hindu Stories'. He may have got them when at Cawnpore, but I find them quaint and charming.

In the Ganges valley fire-flies glitter and flash over tree and shrub, in the evening air and after dark. If you ask a native the meaning of these beautiful and lively flies he will tell you quite gravely. 'You see Sahib there was once a great burglary in Heaven, when the burglars were cast down to earth but obliged, as a sign of disgrace, to carry a lantern in their tail'.

If you ask a native what he thinks the stars are, or what they consider them to be, he will reply 'Well Sahib we say amongst ourselves that they are the holes through which the rain comes.'

Robert Montgomery's last public function in Oudh was to hold a Durbar in honour of a Muslim nobleman, Hurdeo Baksh. The latter had fought against us at Lucknow, but nevertheless had saved, and treated magnificently, all European refugees who, during the Mutiny, had crossed his large estates in the province. The Government of India had therefore decided to confirm on him the title of Raja, and other awards. This was certainly an example of Lord Canning's support for the 'middle way' policy! The occasion was reported fully in *The Times* on 31st March 1859:

The Durbar was held in Mr Montgomery's drawing-room, in which some 15 or 20 chairs were disposed in a horseshoe form before the open door. At 2 o'clock Hurdeo Baksh arrived with a mounted escort and was received by Mr Montgomery, who led him by the hand to the chair on the right of his own. Those present included all the Chief Commissioner's senior officers, his personal staff, the Raja of Kapurthala, with many civil and military dignitaries ... Hurdeo Baksh was dressed in rich robes brocaded with gold, with a cloth of gold overcoat and turban, and cotton socks on his feet ...

All the Durbar rose till the Commissioner and the honoured guests were seated. Mr Montgomery then conferred on Hurdeo Baksh the title of Raja, with an estate in fee worth 15,000 rupees per annum ... Thereafter servants in red and gold liveries brought gifts on trays for the recipient, diamonds, emeralds ... The gift of an elephant with a howdah of solid silver and a beautiful Bombay Arab horse were presented outside to Hurdeo Baksh ... Then the Raja's servants brought in a *nazar* (an offering) of a large sack of gold coin, and placed it at Mr Montgomery's feet ... No wonder, perhaps, that *Baksh* means 'Gift of God'! Then followed a few quiet complimentary speeches that concluded the Durbar and a memorable occasion ...

The Times article ended thus:

Mr Wingfield, the successor of Mr Montgomery as Chief Commissioner of Oudh, arrived in Lucknow this morning ... it is to be hoped that he may succeed in finishing the good work commenced in Oudh by Mr Robert Montgomery.

8
Lieutenant ~ Governor

Murree

23rd May 1859

My dear Brother and Sisters

The mail brought news of the Vote of Thanks to myself by Parliament and of my having been made a KCB! These are indeed great honours and more than half my gratification is the knowledge of the great delight it will give you all. If our parents could have foreseen that their backward, idle, good for nothing son could ever have received such honours, surely they could hardly have credited such a possibility; and the greatest wonder of all age is myself! The Almighty often works with the weakest instrument and He is doing so in my case. To Him alone be the glory. I am now Lt. Governor also, and have been confirmed permanently in Sir John's place . . .

This is a lovely district with a European climate and it is among my many great privileges to be able to reside here in the hot weather; the air is so pure and cool. We have a very nice house for which we pay £160 per annum. Ellen (Lady M) is very well, better than ever I'm glad to say. There are about 150 persons here counting children, and 300 soldiers (Europeans) up from the plains for change of air.

Love from your affectionate brother

R. Montgomery

My grandfather, with Ellen and Lucy (their three-year-old daughter) had left Lucknow on 15th February, but it had taken them a week to reach Lahore as travel beyond the Sutlej was very slow and still largely dependent on the horse-drawn *dak-gari*. At Ludhiana they were met by Mr Elmslie, the Deputy Commissioner, who wrote the following about their visit:

The new Lieut. Governor passed through, wife and child with him, and we had a long talk with the great man. He is old fashioned looking, with grey hair and spectacles, very mild looking and exceedingly gentle in the tone of his voice. He is very kind and polished, and kept up a pleasant conversation for some time. He never forgot any of his visitors. Whenever he thought he had been talking to anyone too long, he used to turn round and commence addressing another.

The so-called mild appearance of Robert was often misleading. People had begun to call him 'Pickwick' because he was outwardly gentle, though, as we have been, he was at times very stern and quite ruthless in getting his own way. It was Elmslie who contrasted the very tough and hard approach of John Lawrence in the Punjab with Robert's policy. 'Sir Robert Montgomery was a much milder, more refined and civilised man, who gradually mitigated the extreme vigour of Lawrence's system.' Apparently Elmslie had suffered a great deal under Sir John, for one of his contemporaries wrote:[26]

Elmslie had imprudently brought a piano with him (to the Punjab). Such refinement was unpardonable and poor Elmslie was moved five times from one end of the Punjab to the other in the course of two years. 'I'll smash his piano for him,' John Lawrence was reported to have said when he first heard of such a degradation as a Punjab officer having a piano!

For the first time in India, Robert was now able to save money, and was evidently not unpleased with his lot. From Murree he wrote on 26th August 1859 to his brother Samuel:

I can save DV £4000 per annum. I am doing so at this rate, and doubt not I shall continue to do it. Never mind giving letters of introduction to people coming out, the more the better; it pleases people at home and gives me no trouble. Sometimes I stand and think, is it possible I am a Lt. Gov., "The Honourable", and KCB?

In India at that time a Lieutenant-Governor was officially styled 'The Honourable' during his period of office. 'His Excellency' was reserved for the Viceroy and Governor-General only. One may wonder how Robert then managed to save annually £4000 (say the equivalent of £100,000 today) - presumably all out of salary and expenses!

My grandfather had not been long at Government House, Lahore, when he heard from London that he was held responsible, and must account to the House of Commons, for that total destruction of the 26th Bengal Native Infantry, when he was in sole charge of the Punjab during the early months of the Mutiny. This was certainly an embarrassing situation, coming soon after his appointment as provincial Governor, his award of the KCB, and the thanks to himself, by both Houses of Parliament, for his 'services in saving Her Majesty's Indian Dominions'!

Robert's reply to Lord Stanley (Secretary of State for India) on this grave charge began very formally:

Lahore

29th April 1859

My Lord

By the most recent intelligence from Home, I learn that the propriety of the punishment inflicted on the late 26th Native Infantry has been seriously impugned in the House of Commons ... On behalf of the Punjab Government I have to thank your Lordship for the considerate manner in which you spoke of the affair in Parliament ... I shall esteem it an additional favour if your Lordship will cause the narrative I now enclose to be laid before Parliament ...

I regret exceedingly to find that a hasty private note of mine, indited under the spur of those terrible moments, has been published and commented on as the deliberate expression of my sentiments. Whilst I have striven to act with vigour against murderers and mutineers, I have never forgotten the duty of Christian forgiveness even towards the worst of our heathen enemies.

I remain, etc.

R. Montgomery

According to Bishop Montgomery the 'hasty private note, indited under the spur of those terrible moments' was in fact the letter of high praise and congratulations which Robert had sent to Cooper, Deputy Commissioner of Amritzar, for his prompt and summary execution of over 300 mutineers of the 26th, two years earlier (see Chapter 5). Somehow this personal letter to Cooper had reached London, and my grandfather now had to justify his actions!

After reading that long 'narrative' (over three close printed foolscap pages) which Robert sent to Lord Stanley, I could not help smiling. For my grandfather is clearly seen not to have given his entire support to Cooper! In his final paragraph he wrote:

Though Mr Cooper s acts may be well vindicated, yet the style of his narrative is much to be regretted ... He omitted to explain fully the necessity which really existed ... His *error* lay not in the act itself, but in the way of describing it; and it is hoped that his countrymen will show a just consideration towards a British officer who evinced great energy and moral resolution ...

Evidently his 'narrative' was accepted by Parliament for my grandfather heard no more of the matter! But he was very nearly sacked, and it was

109

fortunate that Canning was his great supporter and had just written to London about him in these terms: 'Not inferior to any man in his claim to the gratitude of his country is Mr Montgomery, the present Lieutenant Governor of the Punjab. I know but one opinion of the value of his prompt and courageous counsels . . .' However perhaps Lord Canning was also thinking about the 26th Native Infantry, for at the same time he wrote personally to Robert! 'I often think you too sanguine, but I am glad to acknowledge that events have justified you.'

Surprisingly, at about this time, Robert found a new supporter in Sir Colin Campbell (now Lord Clyde) who wrote to the War Office:

> I desire to offer my particular acknowledgements to Mr Montgomery . . . for his cordiality and good will, and co-operation with me . . . The instructions issued by him to the officers under his orders . . . were indeed calculated to facilitate the efforts of the troops . . .

In these circumstances it was quite a relief to find that the career of Mr F. H. Cooper. CB. had not suffered! He became Commissioner of Lahore Division.

In 1859 there were still very few churches in the Punjab of any Christian denomination; the province had only been under British rule for ten years and my grandfather, imbued with all the fervour of his religious upbringing, felt strongly the need to build churches for his British population. What followed is best told in his own words, as given to Bishop Montgomery.

Colonel Reynell Taylor[27], one of the Thomason trainees and a very godly man as well as a great soldier and a noted swordsman, was conducting some Khans from Afghanistan on an official tour of the North-West Frontier, and had reached Sialkot. One of the Khans, noticing a tower, asked what it was:

> 'A church,' said Taylor (Sialkot church was one of the few already built).
> 'What!' the Khan exclaimed: 'Then do you believe in God?'
> 'Why, of course, why do you ask?'
> 'Colonel Sahib, we do not wish to offend but we have always said the English are infidels.'
> 'Why do you think that
> The Khan, with all respect, answered:
> 'Sahib, we have watched you across the border for twelve years. We have fought against you and killed your soldiers and you have killed our young men. But we have always said how brave are the English, what fighters, how honourable, they ever keep their word, we respect them highly. There is one thing that gives us sorrow. They are infidels. They have built wonderful buildings. One thing they never build - a Mosque to their God. Of course they do not believe in God.'

Reynell Taylor realised, presumably for the first time, how incredible it is to the Oriental that anyone could believe in God without showing his belief, every day at all times; reticence on such a matter, so natural to the Englishman, is to him impossible.

Taylor went at once to Sir Robert and told him all. The Lieutenant-Governor was shocked and reported to Lord Canning, asking for the necessary finance so that: 'I can erect a church, however small, in every place in the Punjab where a soldier or civilian is located. For instance in the Derajat, where we have 12,000 troops and four civil stations yet not a single public building devoted to Christian worship.' The Viceroy readily agreed and approved the finance.

This development was in 1860, the year that saw the start of the building of fifteen 'Montgomery Churches', as they became known throughout the Punjab and the North-West Frontier Province. Their construction then cost, in all, 60,000 rupees and the whole work was completed by 1864. There were three categories of church buildings, holding 40, 100 and 250 people respectively; each had its own churchyard and cemetery in which, as the rule of the British raj continued, the headstones of Christian burials increased every year, until Independence came. The Montgomery churches were sited at Gurgaon, Kurnal, Hissar, Rohtak, Sirsa, Gurdaspur, Madhopur, Gujerat, Shahpur, Jung, Mozuffergarh, Dera Ismail Khan (DIK), Dera Ghazi Khan, Bannu and Kohat. Spires and other structural additions were also built for the older churches at Peshawar, Sialkot, Kussowli and Ambala.

I was in the Derajat and attended what must have been the last service in DIK (Dera Ismail Khan) church. Only five people were there though the building holds 100, and it was a remarkable occasion, full of light and sunshine, and memories, though without sadness in any way. The Raj had ended five months earlier, but in that building the Raj lived on - the plaques with the regimental badges on the walls, the memorials to British officers and men, their wives and children, and the Colours laid up in the nave, of an old regiment of Indian infantry raised long ago in the time of 'John Company'. DIK was always a popular and happy station. Until the coming of motor transport, because of the great heat there, it had its own, adjacent, summer headquarters, Sheikh Budin, built on a lone mountain top only 2000 feet above the level of the nearby Indus; but there was no water supply, so every drop of water for this small hot weather station was carried daily to the mountain top by relays of pack donkeys.

In the mid-term of his governorship of the Punjab which then, as we have seen, included all the North-West Frontier Province, my grandfather became much involved in a frontier war. This was the Ambela Expedition and was of particular interest because it was the first time, for over three centuries, that any offensive operation across the Indian frontier into Buner territory had been undertaken. The Buner, a martial tribe of fine

fighting men, whose territory lay north east of Mardan adjacent to Swat
state, were harrassing the border with British administered territory, and
even raiding across it into the Peshawar Division. Robert Montgomery
recognised this situation as one that must be dealt with promptly by
resolute offensive action; otherwise armed tribesmen would break out into
the settled districts, and trouble would spread like wildfire throughout the
North-West Frontier tribes. In his view a military operation was essential
to cross the high and difficult Ambela pass into the Buner Valley beyond;
there the aim would be to sieze and destroy the village occupied by the
Sitana Sayyids (tribal holy men) who were inciting the Buners to defy
British authority, power and prestige.

Robert Montgomery was strongly criticised at the time for his part in
this campaign, particularly for his insistence that it was politically
necessary. Lord Trevelyan, in his admirable book *The India We Left* says
that his great-uncle, Sir Charles Trevelyan, then Finance Member of the
Viceroy's Executive Council,

> distrusted the Lieutenant-Governor, Sir Robert Montgomery. He had heard
> that Montgomery wanted to strike a blow to offset the disturbance to the
> popular mind in the Punjab caused by a Mohammedan prophecy that a great
> event was to take place in the next year. He argued against a proposal to give
> the Commander-in-Chief and the Lieutenant-Governor authority to call up
> reinforcements ... He was opposed to forward operations, which he feared
> might lead to a religious war on the whole frontier.

My grandfather's papers on the Ambela campaign consist mainly of
private letters in their original manuscript. They are exceedingly difficult
to read, some are in very bad condition, and all are tied together with
string, the knot of which is crowned with sealing wax. He must have
thought the collection most important; strangely perhaps there is only one
mention of Sir Charles Trevelyan in the correspondence. There were over
sixty letters to him from civil and military leaders, including Sir Hugh Rose
(C-in-C India), General Sir Neville Chamberlain (GOC Peshawar Division),
General Garvock (Ambela Field Force Commander) and Sir Henry
Norman (Secretary to the Foreign Department in Government of India),
with some telegrams and official dispatches. The senior political officer,
representing Sir Robert and accompanying the expedition, was Major
Hugh James, Commissioner of Peshawar. This was the same (Captain)
James who had been so strongly criticised by Lord Dalhousie for his inept
handling of a murder trial in Peshawar ten years earlier (see Chapter 4)

At the very outset of the campaign Robert sent this almost peremptory
telegram to the C-in-C India:

Telegram from Sir R. Montgomery
To Sir Hugh Rose
12½ am 30th Sept. 63

General Garvock placed the services of the Commissariat at Rawalpindi at my disposal ... Supplies are not procurable in the mountains, everything has to be taken – the distances are short. If you will leave arrangements for supplies and carriage to myself, in communication with the officer appointed to command, the General commanding the Division, and Captain Jenkins, Commissariat, everything will be arranged and provided for, and indeed is now in train. Should there be any difficulty, a telegram will at once be sent to you.

The C-in-C's reply came the next day:

From Sir Hugh Rose
To Sir Robert Montgomery
Recd. 7 pm 1st Oct.

I have received your telegram of the 30th. I leave the arrangements of the supplies and carriage as you propose ... I sanction the concentration of the expedition and supplies at Wabir instead of Nowshera. The Governor General sanctions the use of 2/3 of the cattle and dooli Bearers of Peshawar Movable Column Transport, but a larger proportion are to be used, and even a portion of the cattle and bearers from Rawalpindi, rather than the expedition should *not* take place from want of transport. Acquaint General Garvock of this.

The very next day Robert sent a further (peremptory) telegram to the C-in-C:

To Sir Hugh Rose
10½ am 2nd Oct. 63

It is of the greatest importance to name the troops for the expedition at once ... Otherwise it cannot be ready by the time named by the Viceroy ... Kindly name the Peshawar portion of the force ...
Concerning the plan of operations in the hills I suggest you leave it to the Officer Commanding the expedition, with the civil govt. and the Political Officer. It can only be decided on the spot and there is no time for writing if the Viceroy's orders as to time are to be carried out ... I shall be obliged if you will authorise General Garvock to requisition troops in case of sickness or any other urgent cause ... If the troops at Peshawar are getting sickly it is important to move them out quickly ... Everything is now in train.

After this, troubles began, both over personal relationships and the development of the campaign. On 4th October, General Garvock wrote to Sir Robert:

113

My dear Sir Robert

The Commander-in-Chief's telegram of the 3rd instant gives me full latitude, and I have no time in attending to your request ...

Yours truly

Then Sir Neville Chamberlain became ill (he had been the first commander of the Movable Column during the Mutiny) and the C-in-C wrote to Robert:

The Governor General has sanctioned the arrangements proposed in the event of anything happening to General Chamberlain ...

To increase these difficulties Lord Elgin, the Viceroy, who had succeeded Canning in March 1862, died before the Ambela campaign ended. In this not very suitable climate military problems soon appeared.

By 24th October the column had reached the head of the Ambela Pass, and was hoping to move down twenty miles or more into Buner territory to secure their objective, the village of the *Sitana Sayyids*. But there had been stiff opposition by the tribesmen and the column had suffered unexpected casualties, including British officers, in very hard fighting. Reynell Taylor, Staff Officer to General Garvock, wrote to Robert: 'I believe that things will clear; if not we must adopt some other plan of operations. This opposition by the Buners is an element which we not only did not reckon on, but which from all accounts seemed impossible for them to mount.' At the same time Sir Henry Durand, Robert's old friend who later fell from his elephant at Tank, and a member of the Viceroy's Executive Council, wrote from Calcutta and expressed the hope: 'that the losses inflicted on the Buners were proportionate to our own'.

All in all a very awkward situation had arisen. The truth was that the column was pinned down on the Pass, for the tribesmen occupied the higher ground and commanded the route into their own territory; but to retreat now, as winter approached, would have a disastrous effect on the entire North-West Frontier. For my grandfather in particular this was most embarrassing! His Punjab government were open to a charge of having underestimated the degree of resistance to be expected, and the attitude of the tribes to a show of force by the British.

Clearly reinforcement of the column was essential if it was to attempt to force the Pass, and, as so often happened, six weeks's delay ensued before any decision was taken. During this period the C-in-C wrote a private letter to my grandfather with a proposal so unusual it is worth quoting in extract; apparently he was at Lahore.

114

Private

27 Nov/63

My dear Sir Robert Montgomery
    I am covinced, after discussing with you the operations which would ensure a satisfactory termination to the Expedition, that the best thing I could do would be to proceed to the frontier, and conduct the operations myself . . . !

Yours sincerely
H. Rose

In the event the C-in-C did not 'proceed to the frontier and conduct the operations'. It would certainly have been without precedent! But the column was considerably reinforced and did force the pass into Buner territory, where the tribesmen submitted and gave up the fight. However by this time the C-in-C, still apparently at Lahore on 10th December, had written to my grandfather: 'As we said this morning, the Supreme Govt have given a decided opinion against any invasion of Buner or Swat.' So a political decision followed and Major James negotiated terms with the tribesmen, by which a small 'British Mission' (military and political) marched another fifteen miles to the *Sitana* village, which was duly burnt, and returned to India without incident. Thus honour, for the British, was satisfied, and, as Lord Trevelyan wrote 'the tribes acquired a new respect for the British army which kept the Buner quiet until 1897'.
    But that was not entirely the end of the matter for my grandfather. He had sent his secretary (Douglas Forsyth) to Calcutta, and the latter wrote to him in January 1864 about Sir Charles Trevelyan!

My dear Sir Robert
    I have seen Trevelyan once or twice and yesterday morning breakfasted with him, and had to sustain a vigorous onslaught, particularly from Lady Trevelyan, regarding that 'unholy war' as he calls it. Evidently Lady T has made up her mind that somebody or other is to be impeached and crucified for thus wantonly wasting all Sir T's supplies! The line taken is that there was no real ground for any war at all. But as Lord Elgin actually sanctioned it they think it will be difficult to attach blame to anyone now!

Maybe Robert was lucky? Certainly his career suffered not at all and Sir John Lawrence arrived in Calcutta, as Viceroy, the very day that Forsyth wrote to Robert! Be that as it may, I have written at length about Ambela because it was the *first* frontier campaign undertaken by the British raj after the Queen had assumed government over all India. It was also typical, and indeed set a pattern for the military and political situations so often encountered on the North-West Frontier Province for the next eighty-five years, until Independence came. A typical sequence of events

115

would be - initial fight with tribesmen (perhaps after an ambush), then a column would set out to exact retribution, meeting strong opposition; very hard fighting would take place with sometimes a call for reinforcements. The political agent would become involved and the civil government would intervene. Eventually, fines were levied and tribal villages and towns burnt. It was always exciting, often dangerous, and casualties were not infrequent. Decorations and medals were won, hardships and separation (for all ranks) were accepted without demur. Frontier stations like Waziristan were popular, there was extra leave, and life had a new edge and a new purpose - it was training for war but with *live* ammunition. However, was the policy always right and justified?

My grandfather was never really worried by his Ambela campaign. If he had been he would certainly have mentioned it, as he did most matters, in his letters to his Irish home. About this time he wrote to his two sisters at New Park, Moville:

From Lahore

My dearest Sisters,
    This is the last day of the Mail from Lahore & I, & all of us are *immersed* in business and work. I just write a few lines to say we are all well. Government House has been beautifully done up and furnished, £500 worth of furniture has come from Calcutta and £500 worth of horses (5) will arrive tomorrow or next day, and I have spent on other things some £1000! so money flies faster than I ever knew it go; but every thing had to be got and I suppose I shall get some of it back.
    I am getting well set up & all will be very comfortable and *respectable* if not *grand*. I wish you could peep in and see us. £2000 has been laid out on the house by Govt. It is vastly improved. I am delighted to be in the plains again, and will be very glad 7 months hence to go back to the Hills, we are all creatures of change.
    I find the work very heavy: but I like it & I like a *crisis*. It does me good, I am in one now, imposing new *taxes* on the whole country to make up for our late expenditure; whilst in the other Presidencies they are fighting & butchering I am quietly *doing* it here and in a month will complete the arrangements. If you see me well abused never mind, we must have money & it must be got somehow. The Punjabees are coming down handsomely!

With much love to you all,
Ever believe me
Your affectionate Brother
R. Montgomery

Perhaps the taxes were to pay for the Ambela war!
The seventeen personal and private letters that Lord Canning wrote during his last eighteen months as Viceroy to Robert Montgomery,

covered much of importance for the history of their time in India, and made it very difficult to choose the little that can be included here. Throughout the correspondence Canning's growing affection and respect for Robert is very clear.

On 24th November (1859), Canning writes of problems over the order of precedence of the ruling princes:

I have just seen the proposals for my reception of the Maharaja of Patiala. I cannot consent to it. For the sake of gratifying the Patiala Chief I am to offend another not less faithful feudatory of the Queen - the Jind Chief, who is required to march 120 miles to meet me ... Pray observe that it is not the dignity of Patiala alone that matters ...

Who could tell then that a century later there would be no princes?

Later, on 8th December, Canning discusses, *inter alia*, his forthcoming tour of the Punjab.

I must send you my earliest and best thanks for your admirable management of the license tax ... the highest praise is due to yourself and to those who acted under you .. We leave Calcutta today ... I shall now be at Delhi on 29th and, allowing 21 marches Kurnal to Lahore, with another 10 for stoppages, I shall reach Lahore about 10th February ... After Lahore ... to Sialkot (where Lady Canning will remain) and Wazirabad ... I am most anxious to get to Peshawar if you can organise the means for me; indeed I *will* do it, and shall travel very light, Official and Personal staff at most seven, no escort but such locals and Police as you arrange. I have six carriages, can you cook me up relays of camels, or camels and horses to draw them? Not bullocks or Commissariat cattle!

How long travel took in those days! John Beames, in his *Memoirs of a Bengal Civilian*, provided an interesting sidelight on the trouble taken with this particular Punjab tour, when he wrote about Lady Canning's mirror.

Early in 1860 Lord and Lady Canning arrived. All through the provinces from Calcutta to Lahore the Viceroy had been making a semi-royal progress ... So he came, travelling in a carriage with only half a dozen native troopers as his escort ... Lady Canning, with a similar retinue, followed him. My wife lent her looking glass, the only one in that part of the Punjab fit for a lady, for Lady Canning's use. It was sent on from camp to camp, on a special camel to itself, and did not return to us for many weeks!

Canning's letter ended with the following:

At Peshawar I do not *wish* to meet either the Amir (of Afghanistan), or any of the family. But I secretly desire to avoid the appearance of wishing to escape it

... Dost Mahomed can be told, but not from myself personally, that I shall be at Peshawar, but shall come without any state, simply on local business; if he should desire to send any member of his family to meet me, I shall receive the representative of himself with pleasure ... What do you think of this?

Evidently Canning did not trust the Afghans; if he had agreed to meet their ruler, the latter, in his view, would interpret the occasion as weakness on his part and a tendency towards recession, viz 'the back to the Indus' policy of John Lawrence during the Mutiny, of which Canning was well aware. So many of our Trans-Indus people were of Afghan stock, stretching from Hazara southward to the Derajat.

My grandfather was careful to keep a record of Lord Canning's strong criticism of Sir Charles Trevelyan! This was sent to him by the Viceroy in letters from Simla during April 1860.

When you wrote to me on the 14th you were not aware that Trevelyan's Minute (about Madras taxes) had been published ... Trevelyan has written again, defending his publication ... Pray consider the paper (enclosed) and let me know what you think of it; do not let any other eye than yours see it ... I have no expectation that Trevelyan will resign! There is plenty of obstinacy in him.

Canning's final letter to Robert, on 24th October of the same year, speaks for itself.

Goodbye, my dear Sir Robert. When packing up time comes there will be no man in India with whom I shall more regret to sever my connection than yourself; and certainly none with whom past work and friendship will leave more agreeable and satisfactory recollections ...

The first Viceroy died not long after he returned to England.

It was no surprise to find that my grandfather was well to the fore in controlling policy for recruiting Christian converts to the public service, including the army and police. Furthermore the papers Robert left show how far his views now differed, as a result of study and travel, from the rigid tenets of James Thomason on religious issues. However some senior army officers had not similarly moderated their opinions, and Robert, to his surprise, received a request from General Sir Sydney Cotton, commanding the Peshawar Division, to move one complete regiment to Peshawar 'in order that they might be converted to Christianity'; there was then a strong Missionary College at Peshawar. My grandfather's reply was short and to the point:

On the question of bringing the regiment nearer the Missionaries, with a view to their conversion, my opinion is that Government never would permit their officers to facilitate the conversion of any body of soldiers, and I certainly am not prepared to advise they should be sent to Peshawar.

It was after this incident that Robert thought it right to formalise his views on the extent to which missionary effort *inside* military units should be permitted. He knew well that many officers thought as General Cotton did, and he appreciated the apparent incongruities that existed. Indian Christians were required to join in prayers for the Queen, the Royal Family, the British Parliament ... Yet, Robert wrote, 'we do little, if anything, to support Christians in our government service, who must assuredly have to face the taunts, and boycott, or worse, of their Muslim, Hindu or Sikh colleagues.' My grandfather was often asked at this time: 'May a missionary visit a Christian soldier, or hold a service, in the lines? May a British officer hold a service, or attend a service there?' Against this background Robert issued the following personal advice: 'A missionary may visit his people within the lines, but preaching must be outside the camp. A British Officer ought *not* to conduct any service inside the lines, but may accompany a clergyman who visits his people in the regiment, but *not* if only Christian soldiers are present.' Looking back at Muslim and Hindu regiments in our day, we never dreamt such issues could possibly arise.

In this same connection Robert also had difficulty with his son-in-law Sir Donald McLeod, about whom John Lawrence had written to him: 'Beware of Donald McLeod's religious fanaticism'. McLeod was certainly an extraordinary character. Governed by a belief and conviction that adult baptism was the only baptism, he had himself rebaptised by total immersion - in Lahore. Professionally he was highly competent, though in other ways he often appeared naive and simple. When he became a Lieutenant-Governor (he succeeded Robert) he never had less than twenty horses in his stables, but frequently when he sent for one he found none were available; his guests had taken them! Once he offered security for a nephew for £10,000, but, when the latter defaulted and he was forced to pay up, he nearly had to resign his Governorship, so heavily was he hit.

My grandfather's time as Lieutenant-Governor was by no means wholly a success story, judged from articles about him published in the contemporary Indian press. He was very strongly attacked on several important issues, in the influential *Lahore Chronicle*, the *Pioneer* (Allahabad), and in one Calcutta newspaper. Strangely these attacks were inspired, if not composed, by a member of his own staff, no less than his Judicial Commissioner, Mr Robert N. Cust, who was some ten years younger than my grandfather and highly regarded professionally. He was a noted Orientalist, scholar and linguist. I could not imagine a like situation in our day, unless the critic were sacked instantly, and I read the lengthy articles with amazement, including Robert's handling of the affair;

space allows only very brief, paraphrased, quotation from the newspapers.

On 5th July 1862 the *Lahore Chronicle* reprinted a long article, entitled 'Ad Montem', published in the Calcutta newspaper the *Indian Empire*, which said:

> Behold the iniquity of the Punjab authorities who seek the invigorating climate of the hills, instead of sweltering, *as in duty bound*, amidst the malaria of the plains ... How can we entertain respect for a Lieutenant-Governor who appoints his own nephew his private Secretary and ADC ... the force of nepotism can go no further.

Commenting on 'Ad Montem' the *Lahore Chronicle* added:

> We regard these insinuations against the integrity of the head of the provincial government with disdain ... Having selected a Calcutta newspaper, without circulation in the Punjab, the writer wishes to bring alleged misdeeds to the notice of the highest authority ... It is impossible to identify the writer ...

Ten days later however the *Lahore Chronicle* came out into the open and named Robert Cust as the perpetrator of these attacks:

> It is well known that Mr Cust is a thorn in the side of Sir Robert Montgomery, and therefore the following praise dealt out [to Mr Cust] by the Lieutenant Governor is all the more valuable – 'Your services as Judicial Commissioner have been great; you have wrought important and sound reforms' ... The Lieutenant Governor has always treated Mr Cust with cordial courtesy, and in some important matters, has allowed him a degree of discretion which His Honour would hardly have conceded even to a necessary thorn ... We cannot conjecture the grounds on which Mr Cust bases his antagonism ...

Evidently my grandfather made no attempt publicly to rebuke, let alone discipline, his Judicial Commissioner; instead he loaded him with praise! – perhaps another example of the 'middle way'? I cannot find any reference otherwise to Cust in Robert Montgomery's papers, so presumably there was some personal antipathy between the two men. Cust was a product of Eton and Haileybury, had very considerable literary ability, and was a patron of the arts; his grandfather was the first Lord Brownlow. Robert Montgomery went to Foyle College then Addiscombe, and was essentially a practical man, a hard professional by training and experience; he certainly had no literary ability and his grandfather had owned a wines and spirits business in Londonderry. Surely this wide difference in outlook and social background, character and talents, may account for it all.

Yet that was not the end of the newspaper criticism of my grandfather. The *Pioneer* in Allahabad attacked him strongly on two occasions. When

Cust retired, at the early age of forty-four (he had married three times, had many children, was sick and exhausted) the *Pioneer* said of him: 'Not less sound and useful was the service of his late years in the Punjab, though it may have been less pleasant to a chief who was far from being his equal.' Then, surprisingly, three years later in May 1868, the *Pioneer* resumed their attack on Robert. 'Sir Robert Montgomery strives to think liberal thoughts, but does think loose thoughts; he writes in a slipshod rustic style, which is not normal for high Indian officials . . . If he had remained quiet in England and at Londonderry he might have gone to his grave without having written himself down as a twaddler!'

This scathing reflection on Robert's literary ability affected him not at all, as by that time he was securely settled in Whitehall as a member of the Secretary of State's Council of India! In contrast to the *Pioneer* my grandfather earned most glowing tributes in the *Friend of India*, the journal of the Church Missionary Society. He had been made a Vice President of the Society (so also had Cust!) and one very complimentary testimonial, written after he had left India, again compared him intellectually with his contemporaries:

With the departure of Sir Robert Montgomery India loses a remarkable man. Mr Thomason used to object to the admission of civilians by competition, because, under such a system, we should not have men like Montgomery. In truth he owned little of his success to prolonged study or accurate erudition. But he had the audacity which Bacon declared to be the first, second and third requisites of success. His administration in the Punjab was a period of almost uninterrupted calm and prosperity, *clouded only slightly by the unexpected difficulties encountered in the Ambela campaign.* [The italics are mine!] Above all, satisfied that the time had come when the natives should share more in the administration of the country, Sir Robert established native Municipal Commissioners in the principal cities, as well as Honorary Magistrates.

John Lawrence landed at Calcutta, as Viceroy and Governor-General, on 12th January 1864; his first task was to write to Robert Montgomery:

I arrived an hour ago, all right. Delay nothing for me, let all go on as you have planned . . . I rejoice that the war on our frontier [that Ambela campaign] has been brought to so satisfactory a conclusion. Your letter to me came in the nick of time, as the affair excited some alarm at home and became a very serious matter. I assured the Secretary of State [Sir Charles Wood has succeeded Lord Stanley] that all would go well and be over before I got out – and so it has! The loss of so many officers was a great misfortune, the greatest we have yet experienced on the Frontier since annexation. Still I do not see we could have avoided punishing the Sitana fanatics and their leaders . . . the force employed was very large, and of the first quality; more than equal to that which General Pollock took to Kabul [in the Afghan War] . . . I think what

121

has occurred should be a lesson to us, not to undertake any expedition into the hills, when it can be possibly avoided with honour and safety . . .

This historic letter (not made public till now) shows clearly how my grandfather's Ambela war very nearly brought him down! He escaped unscathed because the expedition succeeded, but the last sentence of Lawrence's letter contained its warning, as well as future policy. It was fortunate too that Robert had friends in Calcutta, from where Sir Richard Temple wrote to him on 11th February telling him that John Lawrence had ordered him to prepare a statement, *defending* the Punjab's financial and administrative performance 'under Montgomery' - against attacks made by Sir Bartle Frere (Chief Commissioner of Sind), and presumably also Cust! There is little doubt that the older provinces were jealous of the Punjab and Punjabi officers; the latter were thought to have unduly favourable treatment, though they came from a recently annexed province, and were still regarded as 'new boys' compared to Bombay, Bengal, Madras, and the North-Western Provinces, and therefore lacked mature experience. Maybe it was lucky that John Lawrence, the Viceroy, was a Punjab man!

Looking back at our country's past imperial and colonial scene the position of a Governor of a Colony or Province often appeared, to regimental officers in my day, to be a most enviable occupation. Residing in Government House in great comfort and some luxury, all free of charge, surrounded by attentive servants and a personal staff always at hand to cope with every problem, with a very full and varied social and recreational life, to which, apparently, you could invite your family and friends - it all looked an idyllic time! However, since reading my grandfather's papers it was clearly not always thus, and snags and difficulties were apt to appear that might quickly unseat you.

Otherwise Robert and Ellen found their last twelve months at Lahore (1864-65) very rewarding and pleasant. Their four sons were all at Harrow, and their youngest daughter, Lucy, was also at school in England. Meanwhile John Lawrence, Robert's oldest friend, had been writing constantly to him for advice and opinion. Robert preserved twenty of these personal (manuscript) letters from the Viceroy, with which he put a printed paper written by himself. This document reflects so well his forward thinking that readers will, I believe, judge it ahead of his time in terms of contemporary policy. An extract follows which shows how percipient was Sir Robert's view of political development in India.

The people should be more largely employed in all social and municipal affairs, which they are most competent to manage. Till quite recently this was neglected, and even now it is very partially done. The appointment of Honorary Magistrates, Municipal Committees, etc., met with opposition from many officers . . .

To do full justice to the people it is indispensable that we legislate with the aid of a Native Council assembled by each Governor . . . At present we know little or nothing of Native feeling . . . Every effort should be made to soften the hard straight lines of our unbending and uncongenial rule, and to adapt it more to the feelings and sympathies of the people . . . to remove the dull sense of restraint and repression, and to afford scope for their legitimate aspirations and love of distinction in our service, both Civil and Military.

In May 1863 Robert and Ellen paid an official visit to Kashmir, lasting five weeks, as guests of the Maharaja Runbir Singh. The *Illustrated London News* of 5th September that year carried a report of this tour with a remarkable illustration (see plate 9) from a drawing by a staff officer, of the meeting between Robert and the Maharaja at the ford in the Jovi River, below the citadel of Jammu. Runbir Singh and Robert are seen reaching out to shake hands from the howdahs of their state elephants, which have halted in the river bed side by side. Behind them are six more elephants for their personal staffs, with a *chhatri-wala* (umbrella-bearer) in each howdah holding up an umbrella to shade his master from the rays of the sun. Only Robert does not have a *chhatri-wala*! At the ford the water is over knee-deep, but the military escorts and guards of honour, including the infantrymen, must stand in the river and present arms, however deep it is; for the official greeting by His Highness of Kashmir has been arranged to take place *in* the river, and not on its shores!

By now the Grand Trunk Road had been completed and metalled from Delhi to Peshawar, a distance of 600 miles; the railway had reached Lahore and was being extended to Multan, whilst steamers were operating on the Upper Indus and plans were in hand for a steamer service on the Sutlej as far as Ferozepore, the river port for Amritzar. My grandfather had even studied plans for the construction of a tunnel under the Indus at Attock - but that had so far not been attempted. All these great developments, including a massive increase in the trade and commerce of the province, were celebrated at the Punjab Fair in Lahore, opened by Robert early in 1864.

In October that year the Viceroy came back to Lahore, his first visit to the province since the Mutiny, for a great reception and Durbar which lasted a week and was a truly magnificent occasion. Robert arranged for the attendance of 604 ruling Princes, who came with huge trains of their followers, as well as the rulers of Afghanistan and Kashmir, the latter with 5000 soldiers. There was a vast camp outside the city walls for 80,000 armed men. The scene was one of elegance and great wealth, with the Princes vying with one another in the splendour and ostentation of their appearance. The Maharaja of Patiala, senior of the Sikh rulers, was blazing with diamonds; Faridkot was clad from head to foot in the true *khalsa* (Sikh) yellow, whilst Jind was dressed in pure white muslin glowing with emeralds and wearing a yellow silk turban. Then, three months later, this magnificent scene was repeated all over again; for a similar Durbar was held on 9th January 1865 to mark the departure of Sir Robert Montgomery from Lahore after six years at Government House. He and Ellen left on the following day by special train for Bombay. From there the journey to England, by sea to Suez (there was still no Suez Canal), and thence overland to Alexandria, now took only two months.

In later years Bishop Montgomery wrote the following:

My father arrived in England in March 1865, and I remember going to London to meet him. I was eight when I last saw him, at Lahore before the great mutiny, and I was now seventeen and a Harrow boy. I expected to see a tall man, I found quite a short one. Moreover I had really to make his acquaintance, and it took years till I respected and loved him; I do not think I fully realised his great merits till I read his record, and he wrote to me so frequently. When he reached London *The Times* published a leading article on his career.

In the time of the British Empire a great proconsul, once he had retired from his service overseas and gone back to live in Britain, often appeared pathetic; he was no longer his country's representative and all the grandeur and trappings of high office were gone. In Robert's case, he had ruled over sixteen million people, in an area of 100,000 square miles, excluding the Punjab states; he had a large salary and never travelled without an escort and his personal staff. His movements were much publicised, even in England, where the *Illustrated London News* of 1864 carried an article describing his camel-carriage, drawn by four camels, which he used extensively; back in London he had to make do with a one-horse brougham.

However Robert and Ellen were very fortunate when they finally returned to London. He was soon made a GCSI (Order of the Star of India) and then appointed a member of the Secretary of State's Council of India in Whitehall. He and Ellen bought No. 7 Cornwall Gardens, a large house near Gloucester Road, in London, where they lived for the next twenty-two years, when not at New Park, our family home in Moville. Those years were a happy and busy time for them and their family, both socially and in official life. When John Lawrence too left India, four years after the Montgomery's, he came to live at 26 Queens Gate, so the two families continued their lifelong association. John was created a peer in 1869 - he was the only Viceroy of India who was not a peer during his time of office.

Later on Sir Donald McLeod retired to London and settled in a small house near Cornwall Gardens, with just his pension to live on. An extraordinary man, he met an extraordinary end. One day at Gloucester Road station he fell off the platform under the wheels of an approaching train, and both his legs were cut off. Robert, and others, were sent for and they told him he had half an hour to live. 'Why,' he said, 'I am perfectly well.' Robert said: 'Are you prepared to go?' He smiled and said: 'Of course' – and died. Another old friend, Field-Marshal Lord Napier of Magdala, also came to live in London, near Eaton Square, and joined this circle of 'Punjabis', who often dined together at Cornwall Gardens. Probably one of the events of those days that most pleased my grandfather was receiving a delightful letter, in June 1870, from the Princes and people of Punjab. This told him that, by public subscription, they had built Montgomery Hall in the Park at Lahore. Montgomery District and Montgomery Town had already been named after him. Much later, Montgomery Hall became the Lahore Gymkhana Club.

In 1877, the year in which Queen Victoria became the Empress of All India, my grandfather fought his last official battle – and lost it! Lord Lytton, then the Viceroy, had decided that the Punjab was too large an area, politically and otherwise, for sound administration. In his opinion it should be divided, by forming a new North Western Frontier Province from the trans-Indus districts. This would leave a smaller Punjab of Cis-Indus territory, with the two frontier districts of Bannu and the Derajat. Robert was furious that anyone should even contemplate carving up his beloved Punjab! He was deputy Chairman of the India Council and wrote a strongly-worded ten-page protest. 'The present Viceroy has been scarcely one year in India, and has only paid one short visit to Peshawar; he can in no sense be said to have made himself personally acquainted with the frontier . . .' But it was of no avail and Lord Lytton won the day!

It is strange that there is no mention in my grandfather's papers of the 2nd Afghan War, nor of John Lawrence's funeral at Westminister Abbey in 1879. Surely he will have been at the latter?

I was also surprised to find no letters to Sir Robert from my maternal grandfather, Dr (later Dean) Farrar. The two men were well acquainted, as Maud Farrar, my mother, married Bishop Montgomery when the latter was Farrar's curate at St. Margaret's Westminster. But probably Robert Montgomery had little in common with the great dean. The latter, a famous scholar, author and educationalist, renowned for his literary achievements, moved in the world of the arts and philology; his milieu was not that of Whitehall and officialdom, though he was so close to it physically.

A letter that Robert wrote to Bishop Montgomery shows how happy he was in his last years, and how fond he was of my father:

My dear Henry
I arrived in India on 13th November 1828. Today, 13th November 1878, I complete a service of fifty years and I am still in harness! How merciful God has been to me. I landed in India not knowing anyone, for I was not at

Haileybury; I had neither talent nor interest. But I was advanced in my career from step to step, and received wealth sufficient for all purposes, as well as honours. A review of the past, thankful as it is, is very humbling – when I took back on the numbers I started with in life, almost all gone, and I am spared. The goodness of God has indeed been great to me, and in the fullness of my heart I cannot help writing a few lines to you.

Robert continued for another nine years 'still in harness'. He was content with his lot, and lived to see his grandchild (son of Henry and his wife, née Maud Farrar), who became Field-Marshal Viscount Montgomery of Alamein KG, GCB, DSO, DCL, DL.

Epilogue

Bishop Montgomery wrote the following in his diary for the 28th December 1887:

This was the day my father died at 7 Cornwall Gardens. I, with others, conveyed his body to Londonderry to fill the last remaining place in the family grave at St. Augustine's Cathedral; as yet ther is no consecrated burial ground at our church at New Park. At Derry we were met with military honours, by the civic heads of the city, the clergy, the gentry, and by a great many of the inhabitants of Inishowen.

Looking back at the broad course of events in India during my grandfather's service, with all the conflicts between differing policies and personal convictions that so beset British rule, one is led to wonder whether this great band of civil administrators and soldiers, of the nineteenth century and later, sufficiently understood their mainly Hindu and Muslim subjects. I may well be taken to task for presuming to write thus, though it is entirely without prejudice to the achievements and beneficial reforms made by Lord William Cavendish-Bentinck and his successors.

The settlement officers (in our day the deputy commissioners) must have got closer to individual village life than any other white men of their time. But the administrators as a whole, the Victorians and the generation that followed, believed they were there, in the final analysis, by right of conquest and the will of God or of providence; they differed amongst themselves, but in the end it was the British who had to be right. They were fortified in this conviction by their knowledge that it was they (the British) who had succeeded in evolving a system of government which persuaded Hindu, Muslim, Sikh, all the classes, to subordinate their religious and caste prejudices, and work together for a foreign ruler. This conviction was strongest in our Indian Army; understandably so in view of its great loyalty to the Raj, with its unsurpassed valour and fighting record, that reached its peak in World War II with the creation of an all-volunteer army of two and a half million men.

All the administrators, such as Sleeman, Thomason, my grandfather, and their successors, were splendid linguists; but does it necessarily follow that they always understood how and why the Indian peasant loved his village, almost before all else? Even in our day he was often content to live in conditions of abject poverty; as a schoolboy he probably could not afford to possess a slate, and therefore wrote on a mud floor with a piece of chalk. He was probably lucky if he had enough to eat, especially when the monsoons failed, and too often his home had no sanitation or independent water supply. As a result dysentry and typhoid were frequent, but there were few hospitals outside the towns or District Headquarters, and qualified doctors were very rare. Nevertheless he thought his village was the most beautiful place in the world, and none other satisfied him.

I believe this was the general picture right up to Independence. Maybe too many of us missed this picture because we did not allow Indians to share in our social life (they were not allowed to join our clubs) and we therefore seldom, if ever, discussed 'village India' with Indians. Above all we were so tardy in our thinking on 'Indianisation'. This began, in the Indian Army, in the 1920s, when two cavalry regiments and six infantry battalions were selected for Indianisation. But the scheme never prospered and, looking back, I recall the sense of innate superiority (certainly on my part!) which prevailed in a non-Indianised regiment at any mention of that 'eight-units scheme', as it was called.

The Indian officers posted to these eight regiments belonged to the educated middle classes; they were all Sandhurst trained and held the King's Commission, just as we did. However their pay was far lower than ours, for we were 'expatriates' who had volunteered to serve in Asia during our professional life, while they were serving in the land of their birth. Therefore they were treated, for their pay, as if they were British officers serving in the U.K.! Yet they were expected to work and live in the officers mess and elsewhere, like all British officers, wear dinner jackets when appropriate, and be content always with British customs, cooking, and menus for all meals. They did join the local station Gymkhana clubs, but few, if any, had either the financial means, or probably the inclination, to apply for membership of the famous clubs of the Raj, such as the Royal Bombay Yacht Club, the Bengal Club, and the like. For British expatriate officers there was always the dislike, or apprehension, lurking in the background, of a future in which one day we, or our successors, might have to serve *under* an Indian officer.

In this setting it was no wonder that the eight-units scheme did not prosper. Later on, in the 1930s, further and more advanced Indianisation was planned; but then, suddenly, the War came and with it urgent demands for modernisation and mechanisation and, above all, the great surge of, expansion of the Indian Army. This literally forced us to begin, and partially complete within five years, the Indianisation measures that we had once thought would take at least twenty years to have any effect. The shock and surprise which the outbreak of World War II gave the British community in India (far-seeing men and women were all too few) was quite extraordinary. In June 1940, when Poland, Belgium, Holland, Norway and France had fallen, and Italy had joined in the war on the side of Germany, the Viceroy and the Government of India, with the Commander-in-Chief and Army Headquarters, were as usual in Simla for the hot weather. The annual summer ball was about to be held - a glittering affair and one of the main social events of the season - and I recall the serious discussions that were held to consider: 'whether officers, this year, should be allowed to wear dinner jackets, and not white tie and tailcoats, which are obligatory for the occasion.' We did wear dinner jackets!

In the event the rapid expansion and Indianisation of the whole army was a great success, and by 1945 there were generally more Indian than British officers in every regiment and corps. At the end of the War I was the last British Commanding Officer of my regiment, and finally I did serve directly under an Indian officer. My battalion was part of the Indian Infantry Brigade involved in the last British offensive operation into tribal territory - the Qghi (Black Mountain) expedition early in 1947. My brigadier had been a student with me at the Quetta Staff College, and later had served *under* me when we were both instructors there. He was a Sikh, we knew each other very well, and all went well where I was concerned; I had seen it all happen!

Against this background, civil and military, I believe the true picture and understanding of the subcontinent did not become clear to the British until near the ending of our rule. We had to wait for our view of the real India, of the villages and peoples of the land, until the appearance of true descriptions by the writers of this century. Philip Woodruff's *The Men Who Ruled India* gave us the picture of government, whilst his *Call The Next Witness* had the clarity of vision which most of us lacked. More recently, modern indian writers have opened our eyes to greater understanding, in works such as *My Village My Life, A Moment In Time*, and the superb *Heat and Dust*[28].

Finally *Plain Tales From The Raj*, widely acclaimed, fascinating, accurate and of absorbing interest, illustrated so well our British attitudes in the twentieth century, before we left. The 'Tales' reveal our professional and social attitudes as rulers, on the face of it intolerant yet in reality the reverse. Shining through it all was our belief that white people were born, and grew up, as superior beings. Did this perhaps limit our understanding, and possibly influence the scale and pace of our efforts, including the money supply, to improve educational standards, urban and village welfare, and alleviate poverty, hunger and disease? I believe the honest answer must be 'Yes', keeping in mind two main facets of British history in India. After Lord Lytton's famous proclamation of Queen Victoria as Empress of India our role as the 'successors of the Mughal Empire' dominated our thinking; certainly in my family we, the British in India, were never wrong. Furthermore the idea that one day our Indian Empire would break up, and that one's career under the Government of India, civil or military, would end, was unthinkable. Personally I held on to this view, perhaps reluctant to accept the inevitable, far too long, until events overtook me!

In practical terms this attitude must have stimulated innate resistance to political and social change. The final sentence in Vincent Smith's *Oxford History of India* speaks for itself. After discussing the various political reforms authorised during Lord Reading's Viceroyalty, the history ends thus:

> A temporary decline in the number of *English* recruits for the Indian Civil Service, which caused some anxiety to the authorities, appeared by the close of 1925 to have been successfully surmounted.

We need now to read the views of modern national historians of India and Pakistan, Burma and Bangladesh. We shall all probably have to get used to a new version of history which may seem very strange to my generation, and of course would have been anathema for my grandfather and his contemporaries. Sir Robert would not have been amused to know that, in the Punjab, Montgomery District and Montgomery Town would one day both be renamed and given their original designation of Sahiwal. But this has happened – it was announced in the 1960s.

Come to think of it, Thomason must have been wrong in his belief that it was God's purpose and will to place India under British rule and protection for all time. Clearly The Almighty was taking a different view!

Appendix

Report in the 'Delhi News' of 19th July 1857 furnished by Ramji Dass of Alipore.

Ramjee Dass of Alleepoor. Went about two months ago to Delhee to complain of being plundered – was confined for a month, and is now released on Security. Gunpowder is made every day, employing two hundred hands – Gun Caps are Scarce. The Cashmeeree Gate is built up with lime. The Nigumbode and other Gates are built up with Stones with the wicket only open. There are about 12,000 or 13,000 fighting men – and about 8,000 fanatics. There is a "Krânnie" in the Bareilly Force. One of the Dehlee Regiments has charge of Salemgurh and the Palace. The Jhansee, Nusseerabad, Rohilkand and Jullundur troops are all encamped between the Dehlee and Ajineree Gates. On the 14th the losses were 1,000 killed and wounded. On the day it rained (9th) none of the fighting force scarcely escaped. The Cavalry are at the Serai or the Delhee Gate, and some are encamped at Durriâgunj, and some at the Bank House and in Begum Sumroo's garden. Some Infantry are in the Shops about the Ajineree and Lahoree Gates. The 60th N.I. and the 74th N.I. are at the Delhee Gate in the shops built against the City wall. In the old Fort there are some Sepoys and two Guns. A Jemadar of the Sappers and Miners has been killed. A Kote Havildar of the Bareilly Force brought the pay of killed Sepoys from the Treasury. The rest of the Force wanted to share the money. He was imprisoned and fined by the King as well as the Pay Master, who disbursed the money – It has been proclaimed that whoever dies in battle, his widow will get 3 Rs monthly pension. The whole population of the City is to be armed. Some magazine Stores have been placed in the Lahoree Villa Bastion. Cow-Killing was commenced, and an affray had occurred – 7 men killed. Now the King's orders are that any one guilty of Cow-Killing will be blown away from a Gun. All the Sikhs and Hindoos had lain down their arms. The butchers were ordered to be arrested, but the Sepoys rushed in and killed them. The Sepoys, and not the King, rule in Dehlee, and all is confusion and riot.

Notes

1 Richard Temple, who later became Lieutenant-Governor of Bengal and Governer of Bombay
2 In the crypt of St. Pauls there is also a memorial plaque to Sir Robert's grandson, Field-Marshall Montgomery. Bishop Montgomery, KCMG, Sir Robert's second son, is commemorated in the Nave in the wood panels on the walls of the Chapel of the Order of St. Michael and St. George, of which he was Prelate for twenty-eight years. Three successive generations of the Montgomery family are thus commemorated in St. Paul's Cathedral. According to the registrar of the Cathedral, no other family in the history of St. Paul's has equalled this record.
3 India Office Library
4 Collector of Taxes, later renamed Deputy Commissioner
5 Mason, P. *A Matter of Honour* Jonathan Cape (London, 1974)
6 Robert Montgomery MSS. (Church Missionary Society Library)
7 Parkes, F. *Wanderings of a Pilgrim* Vol. 1, Pelham Richardson (London, 1850)
8 See Glover, M. *Indian Army Soldiers and Uniforms* Perpetua Press (London, 1973)
9 An Irish earldom which became extinct in 1934. The lovely house, with all its fine old furniture, was burnt down in the troubled times of the 1920s.
10 Mansell, my grandfather's predecessor as third member, recorded how difficult and time-consuming it became to reach any Board decision.
11 Raj, Dr Pragdish *The Mutiny and British Land Policy in North India 1856-58* Asia Publishing House (Bombay, 1965)
12 The author's account is in *A Field Marshall in the Family* Constable, (London, 1973)
13 Government of India Press, Calcutta, 1957
14 Laurie, Col. W. F. B. *Distinguished Anglo-Indians* W. H. Allen (London, 1887)
15 Smith, B. *Life of Lord Lawrence* Thomas Nelson & Sons (Edinburgh, 1883)
16 Sen, Dr *Eighteen Fifty-Seven*
17 Note in Bishop Montgomery's MSS.
18 A reference to Dost Mohammad, the ruler of Afghanistan
19 See also Montgomery, B. 'Lt. Lang's Diary' *Blackwoods* December 1974
20 A paraphrase of the account by Dr Sen
21 See Smyth, Sir J. *Great Stories of the Victoria Cross* Arthur Barker (London, 1977)
22 Outram left Oudh a week after the proclamation was issued

23 Her public proclamation denouncing Queen Victoria's assumption of rule over all India is of course available
24 Robert kept a rough copy of his letter which is almost illegible; his hand writing was always atrocious. Canning's was invariably neat and beautifully clear.
25 Later the Royal Welsh Fusiliers
26 Beames, J. *Memoirs of a Bengal Civilian* Chatto & Windus (London, 1961)
27 At the time he was commanding the Guides at Mardan
28 Mohanti, P. *My Village My Life* David Poynter (London, 1973)
   Pant, A. *A Moment in Time* Hodder & Stoughton (London, 1974)
   Jhabvala, R. *Heat and Dust* John Murray (London, 1975)

Bibliography

Beames, J. *Memoirs of a Bengal Civilian* Chatto & Windus (London, 1961

Cooke, W. *The North Western Provinces of India* Methuen & Co. (London, 1897)

Edwardes, M. *Red Year* Hamish Hamilton (London, 1973)

Glover, M. *Indian Army Soldiers and Uniforms* Perpetua Press (London, 1973)

Jhabvala, R. *Heat and Dust* John Murray (London, 1975)

Kaye, J. W. *Sepoy War in India* W. H. Allen & Co. (London, 1887)

Laurie, W. F. B. *Distinguished Anglo-Indians* W. H. Allen & Co. (London, 1887)

Mason, P. *A Matter of Honour* Jonathan Cape (London, 1974)

Mohanti, P. *My Village My Life* Davis Poynter (London, 1973)

Oman, Sir C. *A History of England* Edward Arnold & Co. (London, 1895)

Pant, A. *A Moment in Time* Hodder & Stoughton (London, 1974)

Parkes, F. *Wanderings of a Pilgrim* Vol. 1, Pelham Richardson (London, 1850)

Raj, Dr P. *The Mutiny and British Land Policy in Northern India* Asia Publishing House (Bombay, 1965)

Savarkar, V. D. *Indian War of Independence (National Rising of 1857)* (London, 1909; Phoenix Press, Bombay, 1947)

Sen, Dr S. N. *Eighteen Fifty-Seven* Government of India Press (Calcutta, 1957)

Smith, B. *Life of Lord Lawrence* Thomas Nelson & Sons (London, 1883)

Smith, V. *Oxford History of India* Oxford University Press (Oxford, 1958)

Smyth, Sir J. *Great Stories of the Victoria Cross* Arthur Barker (London, 1977)

Trevelyan, Lord *The India we Left* Macmillan Publishers (London, 1972)

Index

Figures in **bold** type are illustration numbers (to be found between pages 68 and 69). The abbreviation RM has been used for Robert Montgomery.

135

vii, 2-3, 4, 6; career: commissioned
Bengal Engineers, 4, 90; enters East
India Co. civil service, 7, 11-13; Asst.
Magistrate & Collector, later
Magistrate & Collector, Azamgarh,
13-23; Magistrate & Collector,
Allahabad, 24-37; Magistrate &
Collector, Cawnpore, 40-1;
Commissioner of Lahore Division, 41-
44; member of Board of Administration
(Punjab), 44-5; Judicial Commissioner,
Punjab, 46, 47-88; Chief
Commissioner, Oudh, 88, 89-106;
Lieutenant Governor, 107-26; member
of Council of India, 124, 125
chronology, viii-ix; first marriage, viii,
19; second marriage, ix, 39; furlough
in Europe, 38-9; letters to family, 12,
17-18, 21-2, 61, 63, 107, 108, 116;
religious convictions, 29, 110, 118;
retirement, 124-5; death, ix, 127;
honours: KCB, 107; GCSI, 124;
memorials, 16, xiii, 68; papers, xiv-xv,
79, 105, 112, 132
Montgomery, Robert Thomason (son), 20,
24, 36, 38, 47
Montgomery, Sally (aunt), 12
Montgomery, Samuel (brother), 31, 103,
108
Montgomery, Rev. Samuel Law (father),
1, viii, xiv, 1, 4, 31
Montgomery, Susan Maria (née
McClintock), (Mrs Samuel Law
Montgomery) (mother), viii, xiv, 4-5,
31
'Montgomery Churches', 111
Montgomery District (Punjab), xiii, 125,
130
Montgomery family memorials, 132
Montgomery Hall (Lahore), 10, 125
Montgomery of Alamein, Field-Marshal
Viscount (grandson), 1, xiv, 29, 31, 32,
126, 132
Montgomery Town (Punjab), xiii, 125,
130
Moville (Co. Donegal), viii, xiv, 1-2
Muir, Charlie, 89

Napier, Sir Charles, 50, 51
Napier, Robert (later Field-Marshal
Lord Napier of Magdala), 5, 48, 125;
letter to RM, 68

'New Park' (Anarkulli), 41-2; RM &
family during Mutiny at, 60-1, 64
New Park (Moville), family home at, viii,
xiv, 1, 31, 116, 124
Nicholson, Brigadier-General John, 70,
72-3, 77, 84, 86, 102; and Mobile
Column, 73, 74, 75, 78, 79
Norman, Sir Henry, 112
North West Frontier Province, 41, 111;
RM and Ambela campaign in, 111-16,
121, 122; 'Montgomery Churches' in,
111

Oman, Sir Charles, quoted, 41
Oudh: RM as Chief Commissioner of, ix,
88, 89, 90-106; annexation of, 49-50,
52, 97-8; Canning confiscation decree,
90, 96; settlement plans for, 97;
Durbar at, 105
Oudh, Begum of, see Hazrat Mahal
Outram, General Sir James, 90, 92, 97,
98, 100, 104, 132

Parliament, British: resolution of thanks
to RM, xiii, 107, 109; charge against
RM re 26th Native Infantry
destruction, 108-9
Perkins, Henry, 64
Peshawar; murder of Commissioner in,
48-9; RM at, 49; disagreement with
Lawrence policy for, 75-9
Phayre, Ensign (later General Sir) Arthur,
15, 17
Pioneer, The (Allahabad paper): attacks
on RM, 119, 120-1
Pollock, General Sir George, 30, 32, 121
Pollock, Richard, 40
Pragdish Raj, Dr, 132; quoted, 52, 98
Punjab, 10, 35, 36, 40; annexation &
settlement of, 41; criticism of army in,
59; RM appointments in: as
Commissioner, Lahore Division, ix,
41-4; on Board of Administration, ix,
44-5; as Judicial Commissioner, ix, 46,
47-88; as Lieutenant Governor, ix, xiii,
107-26; life during Mutiny in, 61-2,
63, 64; Canning tour of, 117-18;
jealousy of older Provinces towards,
122; public subscription & letter to
RM from Princes & people, 125; his
protest at proposal to divide province,
125